CHINESE COOKERY

Ella-Mei Wong is an Australian-born Chinese who ever since she can remember was creating some dish, even if it were only on a candle flame in a toy stove. She has lived and travelled in many lands, and everywhere has tasted the food and explored the cuisine.

To the Chinese, cookery is one of the fine arts, and in her book Ella-Mei Wong gives her readers a real insight into Chinese thought on food. And before introducing her delicious concoctions she reveals many of her culinary secrets, telling you all you need to know about the methods, the utensils, and the intriguing ingredients. Simplicity is the keynote of the recipes: they are easy to follow, and the ingredients are readily available, while variations for individual tastes are suggested.

Ella-Mei Wong conducts the Chinese Cookery course at East Sydney Technical College, where the head of the Food School said, "Ella-Mei not only knows how to write about cooking, but she really can cook. I know, because I sample her dishes whenever the opportunity presents itself." She has also published features in the *Australian Women's Weekly*. *Chinese Cookery* will enable still more people to discover the joy and fascination of the Chinese way with food, and particularly Ella-Mei Wong's way.

CHINESE COOKERY

by

ELLA-MEI WONG

Arco Publishing Company, Inc.
New York

First published 1966 in the United States by
ARCO PUBLISHING COMPANY, Inc.
219 Park Avenue South, New York, N.Y. 10003

Library of Congress Catalog Card Number 66-19302

Arco Catalog Number 1476

Printed in Australia

FOREWORD

CHINESE DISHES have become so much a part of the Australian way of life that we tend to forget they are the product of the culture, the tradition, and last but not least the wisdom of an old civilization. Yes—wisdom: long before our chemists, nutritionists, and technologists elaborated on nutritional requirements and procedures, the Chinese excelled in creations delicate to the palate and in devising ways and means of preserving food values and increasing digestibility. Long before raw food and other diets were featured in scientific papers and fashion journals alike, the Chinese knew how to prepare vegetables and keep their freshness, how to use spices and to treat meat.

This book tells the reader not only how to prepare Chinese meals, but what the traditions are that lie behind them: the way in which they are served and consumed, and the occasions when they appear on the table. The author need not be introduced—by her regular television appearances she is well known to the public. She is also a recognized expert on Chinese cooking among members of the catering trade. Many a high-capped dictator of the kitchen has profited from her demonstrations and tuition, and for the past two years she has been teacher of Chinese Cookery at the Food School, East Sydney Technical College.

In publishing this book Mrs Wong does not wish merely to give us a collection of recipes: she has made it a mission to bring closer to us the attitude of her people, who regard life as an art, in which grace is put into every small activity, be it painting a scroll or just making a cup of tea.

D. W. Grover, B.Sc., F.R.A.C.I., F.A.H.C.I.,
1961 Head of Food School, East Sydney Technical College.

PREFACE

MANY PEOPLE ask me the question, "Where should I go to find the best Chinese food?" and I can only truthfully answer, "Your own surroundings are best, with food that you have cooked yourself." My recipes have been written especially for this purpose and are set out as simply as possible. If you follow them carefully, you will soon develop your own individual cooking technique, and in time will become expert in planning and creating your own Chinese menus.

Through travel and through the people of many lands who now live among us, we are coming to appreciate more and more the foods and recipes of other nations. The recipes in this book will, I hope, help you enjoy and understand the distinctiveness of Chinese cuisine.

In cooking as with everything else in this jet age, there are new trends, new shapes, new ideas. Science, too, steps in with new products, such as improved cooking oils, to make food preparation easier and its results more delectable. I have tried to keep all this in mind in writing my recipes. The Chinese ingredients are easily obtainable, and each recipe has been checked and tested personally. I would especially like to thank my good friend Betty Dunleavy for her generous help in this direction.

Also, I should like to say "Thank you" to the many people who had faith in my work and gave me the encouragement I needed to complete this book.

May I wish you happy and successful cooking and may a new culinary adventure be yours each time you use this book.

ELLA-MEI WONG

CONTENTS

Illustrations

THE PHOTOGRAPHS (including the one on the jacket) originally appeared in the *Australian Women's Weekly* (some of them in colour), and I wish to thank the Editor for allowing me to make use of them for my book.

E.-M. W.

1

Chinese Ways and Means

ETIQUETTE

SETTING A TABLE for a Chinese meal, be it formal or informal, is simplicity itself. All that is required is a pair of chopsticks and stand (optional), a deep oval spoon, bowls for soup and rice, plates to stand the bowls on, a small dish for discards, a tiny sauce dish, and a tiny cup with no handle for tea. On a special occasion with a large number of guests, such as a reception, especially if it is held at a restaurant, the tables are set for ten people, and the cost of the feast is based on the number of tables ordered. Each table is served one dish at a time from the menu, which can consist of nine, ten, twelve, sixteen and more courses. In between courses the guests are served wine and can nibble at dried watermelon seeds, and they may smoke. No wonder it takes hours to sit through a Chinese banquet! However, the Chinese feel that by sipping wine and eating alternately, intoxication is prevented to a degree. When congratulations are in order, the host and hostess visit each table and both host and guests toast each other. Instead of napkins, at the end of the meal fragrant warm towels are given to the guests, who find these most refreshing.

In a meal at a Chinese home, all the food is placed on the table at the same time. Plain boiled rice is always served in a bowl (because the depth of the bowl retains the heat longer), and each person helps himself from the side of the dish that is closest to his setting. If a second bowl of rice is required, both hands are used to receive the bowl, as with everything given and received.

Even a simple meal for two would comprise at least two, if not more, dishes. This should be kept in mind when you are planning a Chinese meal.

Tea-drinking plays an important part in Chinese culture. There are many different varieties used as the national beverage, and also consumed for different purposes—for instance, warming-the-system tea; cooling-the-system tea; stimulating-the-senses tea; scented and flower tea; and the sweet-bitter-almond teas. The green or black tea is kept warm day and night, conveniently for the whole family, in a china teapot standing in a padded basket with a lid. Tea is always offered to a visitor, and is served without sugar or milk. Tea has a very delicate flavour and is translucent, and so it is believed that drinking it often will keep the complexion fine and clear. Piping hot tea is served at the end of every meal, so soothing the system after one has eaten.

For a new bride in China, the personal pouring of tea holds particular significance towards her future happiness. After the wedding she ceremonially serves tea to the guests and in return is handed a "lucky packet" wrapped in red paper, the colour symbolizing Joy.

THE CHINESE FEAST

Irrespective of the number of courses on a formal banquet menu, the sequence of introducing the dishes remains the same. They are served in this order: hors-d'oeuvres, two to four small hot entrees, the first soup, eight or more large platters with the second soup in between, whole fish, noodles and/or rice, then dessert. At a birthday celebration noodles would be served along with cakes made into the shape of a peach, denoting "Many Happy Returns", for the peach is the symbol of Long Life.

When seven courses are served it is in honour of a departed soul.

The skill of the Chinese chef is shown by his ability to provide an amazing number of ways to serve the same food, each dish having its own individual taste.

The Chinese do not serve desserts as Westerners know them. Apart from glutinous puddings, rice-flour cookies, sponge cakes, cookies with an almond flavour, darn tarts, and candied fruits, it is usual to serve fresh fruits for the sweet course. And what could be more desirable than the luscious lychee to complete the feast?

EQUIPMENT

Chopsticks

These may be made of wood, bamboo, plastic, ivory, or silver. Those used for the purpose of eating are usually about nine to ten inches long, and those used for cooking are longer and always made of wood. From the top the chopsticks taper down to either a rounded or a pointed end, and this is the end used for picking up food. Both chopsticks must be held a little higher than the middle, and both must be even. The chopsticks rest gently (one on top of the other) between the thumb and the closed fingers—the top stick being the one that moves, with leverage from the first and second fingers. The bottom stick, though remaining close to the top one, rests mainly between the second and third fingers, and is not moved but serves to hold the object to be picked up. When the hold is mastered, chopsticks will do no end of kitchen chores including the beating of eggs, stirring, mixing, and piercing. Either end can be used when cooking so as not to disturb individual flavours.

Chopsticks are easy to keep clean and seldom break, which makes them the most indispensable and economical of kitchen utensils.

The Chinese name for chopsticks, *fai jee*, means "quick brothers", which suggests the quickness with which they can work. Each set consists of ten pairs, and it is traditional to present a Chinese girl with a set upon marriage, hoping she will quickly produce lively and nimble boys.

A great breach of etiquette is to leave chopsticks crossed on the rice bowl. They are never crossed at any time, but are set parallel to each other. The Chinese, ever superstitious, feel that crossed chopsticks are a sign of evil and bad fortune.

At a formal party, a sign to commence is when the host picks up his chopsticks and invites the guests to commence. It is permissible for him to select any particular portion of food from any side of the dish to serve guests, and it is considered quite an honour to be the recipient. In Chinese family life, everyone waits until the head of the family starts before partaking of the food.

The Wock

The French chef reserves a special pan for omelettes, and the wooden bowl for salad would not be used for anything else; likewise the distinctive taste of a Chinese dish stems from the cooking utensils used, the method of preparation, and the exotic ingredients that are added. It is not impossible to produce a magnificent Chinese meal using the equipment already in the kitchen, but for versatility and easy handling the wock is indispensable. It is a pan shaped like a half-circle, with two loop handles attached opposite each other on the rim. It comes in all sizes, with a special seven-inch one especially designed to make skins for spring rolls, and also omelettes. The wock is made of very thin wrought iron or aluminium and it retains the quick heat that is so desirable in Chinese cooking—a quality that must be kept in mind during the cold months if you want the food to be turned out piping hot.

Other Basic Necessities

A ladle with a long handle (wock chan) and one with a scoop to hold liquids (tong hock), a strainer, one or two cleavers, a chopping block, and wooden cooking chopsticks complete the list of main articles required for cooking.

METHODS OF COOKING

Fast Cooking

The methods generally used in fast cooking are chowing, which is pan-frying or sautéing; braising; boiling; and deep-frying—all done in the wock.

Direct Steaming

Hot water is put into the wock, and with the addition of bamboo baskets fitted on top of each other and finally covered with a lid, dim sims, rice dumplings, and steamed bread, both sweet and savoury, are cooked by direct action of the steam. Sometimes a cloth is fastened around the baskets so as to enable the food to cook faster.

Indirect Steaming

The dish to be steamed is stood on a small perforated container and placed in a larger pot with hot water to come within half-way up the side, and then covered tightly with a lid. As the water boils and the steam circulates, the food cooks gently.

Slow Cooking

Large, heavy earthenware pots are placed over a charcoal fire. Since these pots retain their heat for hours, they are suitable for cooking rice, conjee, and medicinal soups.

Barbecuing

The food is cooked over charcoal or hung on hooks in an oven. The well-known red roast pork (char sui), barbecued ducks, and chickens are cooked this way.

PREPARATION OF THE FOOD

Because a pair of chopsticks is the only eating implement (there is no knife to carve on the table), the food must be prepared in pieces which can be easily manipulated,

B

and if food is served whole, such as steamed duck, then it is cooked so tender that it can be easily broken off with the chopsticks.

Ingredients may be sliced, diced, minced, cubed, crushed, shredded, and marinated. The perfectionist strives to keep some kind of uniformity in the size and shape of the ingredients in a dish: for example, if preparing a dish of pork and bean sprouts, the pork would be shredded, and not cubed, because the bean sprouts are long and thin.

There is maximum preparation and minimum cooking in most Chinese dishes, which is of great advantage to the chef and especially to the housewife. Advance planning and preparation of a simple meal or a feast means labour saved, and ingredients can be quickly combined, then bound by subtle sauces and gravies to become delicious offerings. This means there is great economy in the fuel bill, and if the recipe calls for beef or pork to be marinated, then cheaper cuts can be used—they will become more tender and will absorb the full flavour of the marinade.

DRIED INGREDIENTS

Chinese food is known the world over, wherever there are Chinese people living. In this modern age, distance has been conquered by plane travel, which means that goods can be sent to other parts of the world in a short space of time. This is a happy state of affairs for Chinese cookery, because dried ingredients are common in China and used as frequently as fresh or frozen foods, and they do not become spoiled when packed and sent long distances. Therefore any authentic Chinese dish can be faithfully reproduced. Though substitutes can be used for any of the dried foods, the distinctive taste and possibly the appearance will not be quite the same, and so if you are serious about your Chinese cookery and want to produce a truly Chinese dish, try using one or other of the dried ingredients from a Chinese grocery or delicatessen store. There you will see tall bamboo baskets full of odd-looking foods in various shapes, sizes, and colours. These have been dehydrated and need little preparation to have ready to add to your Chinese-style dish.

Here are some of the dried ingredients used in the recipes in this book, and the method of preparing them for a Chinese meal.

Abalone (bow yee) : Brownish red in colour. These need to be soaked in warm water overnight. Wash thoroughly to remove any sand, scrubbing with a small brush if necessary. Used as an appetizer and in soup. Abalone is used in an authentic Chinese braised dish.

Bean curd (foo jook) : This is sold in sticks or sheets. soak in warm water for 10 to 15 minutes. It has little flavour of its own, but it is highly nutritious and is served with other foods to absorb their flavours. Used in soups and braised dishes—the latter are served on days of fasting.

Bird's-nest (yin wor) : Soak in water overnight, then cleanse thoroughly and use tweezers to pluck away any tiny feathers that may have become stuck to the gelatine-like bird's-nest. Used in soup and considered a necessary delicacy in any banquet menu. When sweetened, it is served as a dessert.

Fungi (chee yee) : Greyish-black in colour and wrinkled. When soaked in cold water for 15 minutes they expand to their fullest extent, and have an elastic-like quality. Wash well and use in numerous dishes where they can absorb the flavour of richer foods.

Lotus root (lin kno) : Soak in hot water for 30 minutes. Used in soup, and when candied it looks attractive, for it has a natural perforation.

Lotus seeds (lin jee) : Cover with hot water and soak for one hour.

Mushrooms (doong gwoo) : Obtainable in Far Eastern countries (the best ones are supposed to come from Japan) . They are grey to black in colour and come in varied thicknesses—from thick-centred mushrooms (considered first grade) to thin ones that are split on the edges and resemble a flower. They are available in sizes from very small to large. Soak all types in warm water for 20 minutes, when they will expand to their fullest extent. Wash and clean thoroughly, then soak in a second bowl of water, which can be retained and used as stock. When ready to use, squeeze the mushrooms dry and remove the stems (these can also be used in the stock-pot) .

Oysters (hor see) : Soak in warm water overnight. Wash thoroughly. They are used in soups and braised dishes, and also as a substitute for fresh oysters, though they have a different flavour altogether.

Red dates (hoong joh) : Soak in hot water for 30 minutes or longer. These dates are sweet-tasting and about $\frac{3}{4}$ inch in length. They have an elongated seed. Red dates are used in soup and steamed dishes.

Scallops (gong yo jee) : Soak in warm water for eight hours, when they will be easy to pull apart in shreds. Used extensively in soup and omelettes, and can also be eaten as they are, for an appetizer.

Shark fin (yee chee) : Wash thoroughly and soak overnight if in its original state, removing any black skin. When purchased loose, it is only necessary to soak for a few hours. Shark fin is the supreme delicacy on a banquet menu.

Shrimps (har mei) : Soak in warm water for one hour or longer; these are used as a substitute for fresh shrimps, but are inclined to be on the salty side. They are most desirable for use in omelettes and soups.

Squid (yew yee) : Soak in warm water for one hour or longer. Wash thoroughly, removing any sand and taking particular care to clean the tendrils. Peel off the skin and cut a criss-cross pattern on the inside. When cooked, the squid will curl into a patterned log shape which is quite attractive. They are excellent fare when steamed and are used in dishes combined with vegetables.

THICKENING AGENTS

Lotus flour (lin fun) and chestnut flour (mar tay fun) are derived from the lotus and the chestnut respectively and are used as thickening agents in Chinese cookery. Other such agents would be sago, tapioca, and potato. For convenience cornflour, arrowroot, and plain flour may be used instead.

SAUCES AND SEASONINGS

Chilli sauce: There are many grades of fierceness among the various brands of chilli sauce. It is used as a dip sauce.

Five-spice: Obtainable in small packets, this consists of a mixture of five spices. The main ones are Chinese aniseed, cloves, cinnamon, anise herb, and the aromatic seeds of fennel. The spice imparts a wonderful aroma to food.

Fresh green ginger: The young root of a tropical plant, this is used extensively in Chinese cookery. It has the ability of masking fishy odours when used in seafood cookery. When out of season it can be bought in tins.

Garlic: In form garlic is a bulb similar to an onion, but it can be broken away in separate cloves. It can be chopped finely, crushed, or pressed to release the juice, and is used to flavour Chinese dishes.

Hoysin jeung: Obtainable in tins. This is made of bean flour and spices, very rich in flavour and colour. It is easy to become accustomed to its taste.

Lemon sauce: A lemon chutney used as an accompaniment for red roast pork or barbecued duck.

Monosodium glutamate: This is marketed under various trade names. It is of vegetable origin, and used very sparingly and with discretion it enhances the natural flavour of foods. The Chinese version is a fine white powder called Ve-Tsin. In Australia it is known as Zip.

Oyster sauce: Made from Chinese oysters, this sauce imparts an exotic and individual flavour. It gives distinction to any dish and is obtainable in bottles. There are different degrees of strength.

Red bean curd: A soy bean product, obtainable in tins. The red colour is added.

Rice wine: Made from rice, and is very similar to sherry.

Sesame oil: A highly refined fragrant oil obtained from the sesame seed. It keeps indefinitely. Mainly used for flavouring food.

Soy sauce: Made from salted and fermented soy beans. No Chinese kitchen is ever without it. There are different grades, ranging from thin to thick, and the colour varies from light brown to dark reddish brown. It may be used during the cooking process and is always set on the table as a dip sauce, just as salt and pepper would take its place on a Western table. Though salty, soy sauce is not a complete substitute for salt.

Shrimp paste: This is made from tiny shrimps and it takes thousands to make up one small bottle. As this paste has a strong fishy odour and is purplish in colour, one has to acquire a taste for it. It is used very sparingly in conjunction with other dishes. A small dish steamed while the rice is cooking is served as an appetizer to the lovers of this paste.

Taofu: Made from soy bean curd, a similar texture to soft cheese. It has no flavour of its own, but is highly nutritious. It is usually cut into blocks about one inch by three inches. In its fresh state it has a milky colour and is also cut into one-inch cubes and deep-fried.

White bean curd: Made from soy bean, salted and used as an appetizer or with vegetable dishes.

COOKERY TERMS

Barbecued: Generally means cooked over an open fire or charcoal burner over coal.

Basted: Liquid is spooned or brushed over the food that is being cooked.

Blanched: Plunged into boiling water for a given period of time.

Braised: Browned in a little oil or lard, then cooked over low heat with a small amount of water or stock.

Crushed: Pounded or crushed with a cleaver.

Cubed: Cut into cubes ($\frac{1}{4}$ inch to 1 inch).

Deep-fried: Cooked in enough oil to cover food to be fried.

Diced: Cut into $\frac{1}{4}$-inch cubes, or even smaller.

Drippings: The juices that remain from the cooked food.

Garnished: Something added to decorate the finished product.

Marinade: The liquor left after food has been marinated.

Marinated: Soaked in a marinade—usually soy sauce, oil, vinegar and seasonings. The purpose of this is to make the food more tender and to impart a special flavour.

Minced: Chopped very finely with two cleavers, or put through a mincer.

Mixed: Stirred together.

Pan-fried: Cooked over heat in a little oil or lard.

Parboiled: Partially boiled.

Sautéd: Cooked quickly over heat in a little oil or lard (turning frequently). It means literally jump from the pan.

Shredded: Cut into very thin strips (1 inch to 1¼ inches in length).

Simmered: Cooked over low heat just under boiling point.

Sliced: The food is cut into thin oblong pieces either diagonally or straight across (in size 2 inches by 1 inch). Used mainly for the Chinese chafing dish known as sukiyaki, and for hard vegetables.

Soaked: Covered completely with liquid for a specified time.

GLOSSARY OF CHINESE TERMS

These spellings give the nearest phonetic approximation to the actual Chinese words.

Bie: Presenting or decorating food after it has been cooked; serving food with a garnish to attract the eye.

Bo: The process of boiling, as in bo farn or boiled rice.

Chow: Frying quickly in a little oil or lard in a shallow pan, when the ingredients literally jump from the pan; to toss food.

Dunn: Slow cooking in a large earthenware pot over a charcoal fire; for instance, a whole duck would be simmered for hours in this way.

Gook: Baking in an oven.

Gup: The ingredients are first sautéd, then braised in stock and simmered until tender.

Heung sui: A barbecue process which colours the food after it has been seasoned, usually with a thick soy sauce to give it a deep, rich brown colour; a fragrant grill.

Hong: Toasting or grilling.

Jar: To squeeze or extract liquid.

Jeng: The food is placed in a casserole, then on a stand in a large pot of boiling water, and covered with a lid, then allowed to steam gently.

Jow: Frying in sufficient oil or lard to deep-fry.

Jin: Lightly fried in butter or oil; the term applied to frying a whole egg.

Jum: Placed in water or liquid to either soak or marinate.

Jup: A sauce or gravy of varying textures; drippings from cooked meats.

Yeung: Ingredients are minced or finely chopped to be stuffed in a vegetable or fish.

Yip: To pickle fruit and vegetables, or to salt fish.

2

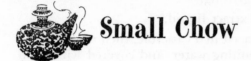 Small Chow

THE CHINESE have savoury and sweet titbits called *deem sum*, and the deem sum hour is generally between the first meal of the day and midday. The popular *dim sim* sold in food shops at the same counter as the meat pies and hamburgers is only one of the deem sum group, which includes various small steamed patties and buns with different fillings, and assorted shapes, pastries, and other tasty titbits. All these are ideal for a hors-d'oeuvre at a westernized cocktail party, and give the party an oriental touch. At a formal dinner party or an official function, watermelon seeds, candied fruits, dried abalone, jellyfish, Chinese salami, preserved eggs, or cold small meats may be served as a hors-d'oeuvre before the main dish is brought to the table.

When deem sum are served in a Chinese restaurant each order comes in its own individual bamboo container or tray, and after the customer has consumed the various dishes of his choice, the cost of the repast is calculated on the number of empty bamboo trays stacked beside him. Service of deem sum is obtained by calling the waitress, who walks around nonchalantly with her special wares.

The recipes that follow are just a few of the delicious titbits that the Chinese class as small chow.

SHRIMP BREAD
MIN BOW HAR

½ lb. raw shelled shrimps   Salt
1 onion   1 dessertspoon sherry
1 egg   Slices of stale bread
1 tablespoon soy sauce   Oil for deep-frying

Mince shrimps together with onion. Add unbeaten egg white, soy sauce, salt, and sherry. Cut stale bread into one-inch squares or shapes, pack shrimp mixture on to them and dip in beaten yolk of egg. Heat oil and deep-fry until golden brown, with the shrimp side facing downwards. Drain.

CHICKEN LIVERS
GAI GEN

Chicken livers   A pinch of baking powder
2 tablespoons soy sauce   3 tablespoons water
1 tablespoon sherry   Oil for deep-frying
½ cup plain flour   1 tablespoon salt-pepper
                            mixture

Cut livers into ¾-inch pieces and marinate in soy sauce and sherry for 10 minutes. Mix flour, baking powder, and water into a paste and dip chicken livers into it. Deep-fry in hot oil, drain, and serve with salt-pepper mixture.

Salt-pepper mixture: Heat ¼ cup salt and 2 teaspoons black pepper together for a few minutes. When cool, store in a shaker.

SHRIMP BALLS
HAR YIN

1 lb. raw shelled shrimps   1 egg white
2 teaspoons soy sauce   Oil for deep-frying
½ teaspoon salt

Shrimp Balls—*Continued*.

Mince cleaned shrimps and season with soy sauce and salt. Beat egg white until stiff and fold in shrimp mixture. Heat pan and add enough oil to deep-fry teaspoonfuls of the mixture. Drain when brown. These may be served on skewers.

CHINESE SALAMI
LARP CHOONG

Cook one pair of Chinese salami (pork or liver) by the indirect steaming method for 20 minutes. When cool, cut into diagonal slices. Or steam on top of the boiled rice when it is at the simmering stage.

SLICED ABALONE
BOW YEE

Abalone available in a can, plain or in soy sauce, sliced on the bias and served with a sprinkling of lemon juice.

SHRIMP CRISPS
HAR BEANG

¼ lb. shrimp crisps   Salt
Oil for deep-frying

Heat enough oil to deep-fry, and when hot, drop in shrimp crisps. If the oil is at the correct temperature the crisps will float to the top and double in size. Drain and serve with a sprinkling of salt.

THOUSAND-YEAR-OLD EGGS
PEE DARN

For the preparation of these eggs see page 36. Peel off coating and shell the eggs. Cut into wedges and serve with vinegar and preserved ginger shreds.

PRAWN APPETIZERS
DAI HAR YIN

½ lb. raw shelled prawns
Salt
1 teaspoon soy sauce
1 egg white

1 teaspoon cornflour
Oil for deep-frying
1 inch green ginger, crushed
Lemon

Clean prawns and mince with salt and soy sauce. Mix in egg white and sprinkle with cornflour. Fashion into little balls and deep-fry until brown in hot oil to which the ginger has been added. Drain and serve with lemon juice.

FRIED WUN TUN
JOW WUN TUN

Fine noodle paste cut into
2½-inch squares
½ lb. pork (not too lean)
6 raw shelled prawns

Salt
1 teaspoon sugar
2 teaspoons soy sauce
Oil for deep-frying

Mince pork and prawns together. Season with salt, sugar, and soy sauce. Place ½ teaspoon of this mixture in a noodle paste square, fold it in securely and deep-fry in hot oil. Drain. The mixture can be varied with onion, meat mince, bamboo shoots, or water chestnuts.

3

 Meats

PORK is the most popular meat in China. Strange as it may seem, the parts considered unwanted on a westernized table, such as the kidneys, stomach, feet, and tail, are the most expensive. A delicious and nourishing thick rice broth called conjee, made with the kidneys and stomach, is consumed as freely as an afternoon tea cake. The pork fillets are marinated in a red bean sauce and highly seasoned to become the well-known barbecued red pork or char sui, which is the authentic base of any fried rice dish. Again, the skin is not wasted, but cooked to advantage together with the pork; the rib bones are made into dishes with salty black beans, pungent sauces, and barbecued to perfection. Chinese smoked hams are always found hanging in the special shops that sell cooked meats, and it is possible to buy small portions of any food even to eat on the spot. Owing to the fact that land in China is usually considered too valuable for pasture, there is not a great deal of cattle-breeding carried on; consequently beef is expensive. But whereas recipes in the past called for small quantities of beef just to flavour the dish, it is different now, because much beef is imported into China, and the Chinese are fond of the flavour, so that many dishes have been adjusted to make allowance for this change.

Mutton is used more in the north of China, and a barbecued skewer of mutton is a common sight. In Cantonese cooking, mutton is never used in the stock-pot, the preference going to chicken bones or pork bones.

Sarm Sare Oiu Gai is the winter delicacy to keep the body warm. It comprises three snakes—one carpet and two black snakes which are specially kept for this purpose— and a chicken. There is no recipe for this!

SWEET-SOUR PORK
SIN TIM JEE YUK

1 lb. lean pork	1 egg yolk
1 tablespoon sugar	Cornflour
1½ tablespoons soy sauce	Oil or lard for deep-frying
Salt	1 large onion
½ teaspoon monosodium glutamate	1 carrot
	1 green pepper
1 tablespoon sherry	½ cup pineapple pieces

Cut pork into cubes (about ¾ inch). Put them in a mixture of sugar, soy sauce, salt, monosodium glutamate, and sherry; let stand for 20 minutes. Add egg yolk, mix well. Roll each piece of pork in cornflour and deep-fry in hot oil until almost cooked. Drain and re-fry, then place on a platter. Cut vegetables into cubes. Cook the onion in a little oil until soft, then add the carrot which has been par-boiled and green pepper. Pour over sweet-sour sauce, mix in pineapple pieces, and serve over pork.

Sweet-sour sauce: Combine ½ cup vinegar, 3 table-spoons sugar, ½ teaspoon salt, 2 teaspoons tomato sauce, 1 inch green ginger, and 1 cup pineapple juice and bring to the boil. Blend 2 teaspoons cornflour with a little warm water, add to mixture, and cook for one minute, stirring all the time. If preferred, remove green ginger before serving.

PORK WITH FUNGI
JEE YUK CHOW CHEE YEE

1 lb. pork	½ teaspoon monosodium
1 oz. fungi (chee yee)	glutamate
1 large onion	Oil
4 stalks celery	1 clove garlic, crushed
2 tablespoons soy sauce	1 inch green ginger, crushed
2 teaspoons sugar	2 teaspoons cornflour
Salt	½ cup stock
	1 teaspoon oyster sauce

Soak fungi in hot water for 20 minutes, then wash and rinse it. Peel and slice onion, and slice celery stalks crosswise. Cut pork in the same fashion and mix it with soy sauce, sugar, salt, and monosodium glutamate. Heat oil in pan, add garlic and ginger and sauté onion. Add pork and cook until nicely browned. Add celery and fungi, mixing well together, and cook for another minute. Make a smooth paste with cornflour and warm water, add stock and oyster sauce, pour into mixture and cook until thickened, stirring frequently.

SKEWERED PORK
JEE YUK SARTEE

½ lb. lean pork	A pinch of chilli powder
½ cup grated nuts or peanut butter	½ teaspoon cinnamon
	Soy sauce
½ teaspoon salt	Oil

Make a smooth paste of grated nuts, salt, chilli powder, and cinnamon. Moisten with soy sauce. Cut pork into one-inch cubes, rub the nut paste on, then pound in with the back of a wooden spoon. Let stand for 15 minutes. Thread a skewer with five or six pieces of pork and cook under a hot griller; baste with oil while cooking.

*For a luncheon treat serve as the main dish Pork Chow Mein.
The side dishes are red and golden brown ginger in syrup,
and a spicy chutney. Serve also a clear soup with Chinese
spinach and minced ham added. Almond cookies and fresh
navel oranges give a final touch to this superb meal.*

Skewered Pork (Jee Yuk Sartee) comprises cubes of pork threaded on skewers, served on a bed of steamed rice, with crisp-textured bean sprouts. Accompany with a dip sauce of chilli, mustard, or soy sauce.

MUSHROOM CUPS
YEUNG DOONG GWOO

2 dozen medium-sized mushrooms
½ lb. ground pork
2 slices cooked ham, minced
1 egg white
10 water chestnuts, chopped
Salt

2 tablespoons soy sauce
2 teaspoons cornflour
2 tablespoons oil
1 tablespoon sugar
1 tablespoon sherry
2 tablespoons stock
Capsicums

Prepare mushrooms by soaking in hot water for 20 minutes. Combine pork, ham, egg white, and chestnuts,
season with salt and soy sauce. Sprinkle with cornflour
and mix well together. Heat pan, add oil, and sauté
mushrooms for 2 minutes with sugar and sherry. Remove
and allow to cool. Pack mixture on to each mushroom
(inside) and decorate with a strip of capsicum across
centre. Place in a shallow bowl and steam for 15 minutes.
Now pour over stock, and allow to steam for a further
10 minutes. Serve with a dip sauce made from soy sauce and
sesame oil.

RED ROAST PORK
HOONG CHAR SUI

2 lb. pork fillets
4 tablespoons soy sauce
2 teaspoons thick red sauce
(hoy sin jeung)
2 teaspoons five-spice (heung
lo fun)

2 tablespoons sugar
Salt
A piece of green ginger,
crushed
1 clove garlic, crushed

Combine sauces, sugar, salt, ginger, and garlic in a bowl.
Brush this over the pork fillets and let stand for 30 minutes. Roast in a hot oven—about 425 degrees—for 15
minutes, then reduce heat to 350 degrees and cook for
approximately 30 minutes. Remove. Cut into slices
diagonally and serve with lemon sauce (nim noong
jeung) or Chinese plum sauce.

C

FRIED CRISP PORK
JEE JOW YUK

1 lb. fresh belly pork	2 tablespoons sugar
3 tablespoons soy sauce	2 cups stock
2 teaspoons sherry	1 egg
1 petal dried aniseed (bark gock)	1 cup cornflour
	Oil for deep-frying

Season pork with soy sauce, sherry, dried aniseed, and sugar. Simmer in stock until soft. When cool, cut pork into pieces about ¼ inch thick and 2 inches long and dip into combined egg and cornflour. Deep-fry in hot oil until brown.

SPICED PORK
KO YUK

1½ lb. fresh belly pork	1 clove garlic, chopped
2 tablespoons soy sauce	1 tablespoon sherry
Salt	Oil for deep-frying
A piece of green ginger, crushed	3 tablespoons preserved vegetable (doong choy)

Reserve any bones for soup or spare ribs. In a saucepan boil enough water to cover the pork, immerse the pork in it for 2 minutes, then plunge the pork into a second saucepan of cold water. Repeat the process four or five times. Remove and drain. Combine soy sauce, salt, ginger, garlic, and sherry in a bowl, and rub on both sides of the pork. Let stand for 25 minutes. Heat oil in a deep saucepan and deep-fry the pork, skin side down, over low heat, until the skin is crisp. Remove, and when cool, cut into slices about 2½ inches in length and ¼ inch thick. Arrange in a shallow bowl with the hard skin facing downwards; pack preserved vegetable on top, and steam for 30 minutes. Serve with flat rice noodles.

BEEF CHOP SUEY
KNO YUK JUP SUI

1 lb. beef
3 tablespoons soy sauce
Salt
½ teaspoon monosodium
  glutamate
1 tablespoon sherry
2 stalks Chinese cabbage, or
  cauliflower

1 large onion
2 stalks celery
½ lb. beans
Oil
2 slices green ginger
1 clove garlic, crushed
1 tablespoon cornflour
1 cup stock

Slice meat and marinate it in a mixture of soy sauce, salt, monosodium glutamate, and sherry. Slice vegetables and parboil beans. Heat pan, add oil, ginger, and crushed garlic. Sauté vegetables and remove. Add more oil to the pan and sauté meat until it browns, return vegetables and mix well together, cooking for a further minute. Add marinade, blended cornflour, and stock. Cook a further minute or two and serve with plain boiled rice.

STEAK SLICES AND GHERKIN
JING CHAR GWAH YUK

¾ lb. round steak
1 inch green ginger, sliced
1 tablespoon soy sauce
Salt
1 teaspoon cornflour

4 pieces preserved gherkins
  (char gwah)
1 tomato, skinned
1 teaspoon sesame oil
1 teaspoon sugar
Chopped shallots

Slice meat and put it into a bowl with green ginger, soy sauce, salt, and cornflour. Marinate for 20 minutes. Slice gherkins and cut tomato in four. Prepare a deep bowl for steaming and place in gherkins, then the meat slices and marinade. Pour over the sesame oil and place the tomato on top. Sprinkle with sugar and steam for 20 minutes. Just before serving, add chopped shallots.

ASPARAGUS WITH BEEF
KNO YUK CHOW LO SOON

1 lb. beef
Salt
2 tablespoons soy sauce
Cornflour
2 cups cauliflower
1 small bunch fresh
  asparagus or 1 small tin
  asparagus

Oil
1 tablespoon sugar
1 clove garlic, crushed
1 cup stock (or liquor from
  asparagus)
1 tablespoon sherry
2 tablespoons oyster sauce

Cut beef into strips and season with salt and soy sauce. Sprinkle with cornflour. Mix well together and let stand for 15 minutes. Cut cauliflower into flowerets and blanch for one minute. String asparagus and cut diagonally in 1½ inch lengths. Heat pan, add oil, and sauté asparagus for one minute. Add salt, sugar, water to cover, and simmer until soft. Drain and reserve liquid. Heat pan, add about 1 tablespoon oil and the garlic. Sauté beef until it browns, then put in vegetables and stock and simmer for one minute. Thicken with blended cornflour and add sherry and oyster sauce, cooking a further minute or two.

If using fresh oysters in place of oyster sauce, put the oysters in a grinder and heat with liquor until it reaches boiling point. Add salt to taste. Strain.

CATHAY STEAK AND ONIONS
KNO YUK PAR

¾ lb. lean steak
1 tablespoon soy sauce
1 teaspoon sugar
1 inch green ginger, crushed
1 clove garlic, crushed
Salt

Oil
2 medium-sized onions
1 tablespoon cornflour
1 tablespoon water
2 teaspoons oyster sauce
½ cup stock

Marinate sliced meat in soy sauce, sugar, ginger, garlic, and salt for 15 to 20 minutes. Heat pan, add oil, and

Cathay Steak and Onions—*Continued.*

sauté sliced onions until soft. Add a little more oil and put in meat. Stir briskly and cook until meat is well seared all over. Make a smooth paste with cornflour and water, add oyster sauce and stock, pour into meat mixture, and cook for a further minute.

STEAMED STEAK WITH ASPARAGUS OR TOMATOES
JING KNOW JUK

$\frac{1}{2}$ lb. coarse minced steak	Salt
2 tablespoons soy sauce	1 inch green ginger, crushed
1 teaspoon sugar	1 teaspoon cornflour
$\frac{1}{2}$ teaspoon monosodium glutamate	1 tin asparagus, or tomatoes
	1 teaspoon oil

Place minced steak in a deep bowl and marinate in a mixture of soy sauce, sugar, salt, monosodium glutamate, ginger, and cornflour. Leave for 20 minutes. Put water in a deep saucepan, and when boiling place the bowl of steak on a stand so that the water comes about half-way up the bowl. Steam for 25 minutes. If using asparagus, about 5 minutes before the minced steak is cooked place the asparagus on top of it and then pour over the oil. (If using tomatoes, do this 15 minutes before cooking time is up, adding sugar and oil to taste.)

STUFFED MEAT BALLS
YEUNG YUK YIN

6 hard-boiled eggs	2 large onions
Salt	Oil
2 tablespoons soy sauce	1 teaspoon cornflour
1 lb. minced beef	$\frac{1}{2}$ cup water
2 tablespoons tomato paste or tomato puree	1 tablespoon sherry

Quarter hard-boiled eggs when cool. Mix salt and half the soy sauce with minced beef and a little of the tomato

Stuffed Meat Balls—*Continued.*

paste. Mince one onion and add to the beef mixture. Cover each piece of egg with meat mixture. Heat pan, add a little oil, and brown the eggs all over. Chop the other onion finely and fry in a little oil until well browned. Blend cornflour with water and add remaining soy sauce, sherry, and remainder of tomato paste. Place meat balls in, and simmer until cooked (about 15 minutes) over very low heat.

PINEAPPLE MEAT BALLS
BOR LOR YUK YIN

½ lb. steak	¾ cup pineapple juice or stock
1 large onion	
Salt	1 cup pineapple pieces
1 tablespoon sherry	1 tablespoon soy sauce
1 egg white	½ cup vinegar
Cornflour	½ cup sugar
Oil for deep-frying	Lengths of shallots

Mince steak and onion together and add salt and sherry, then mix in egg white. Make into small balls about 1½ inches in diameter, roll in cornflour, and deep-fry in hot oil until they turn brown. Remove excess oil and simmer with stock or pineapple juice for 2 or 3 minutes. Add pineapple pieces. Blend 1 tablespoon cornflour, soy sauce, vinegar, sugar, and salt. Stir thoroughly into the mixture. Garnish with lengths of shallots and cook for a further 3 minutes.

BRAISED FLANK STEAK
MUN BARR NARM

1 lb. flank or skirt steak	1 clove garlic, crushed
A piece of preserved Chinese vegetable (choong choy)	A piece of green ginger, crushed
Oil	1 petal aniseed (bark gock)
Salt	1 small stick cinnamon

Braised Flank Steak—*Continued.*

Wash and separate the Chinese vegetable and cut into small pieces. Cube skirt steak into one-inch pieces. Heat pan, add oil, salt, garlic, and ginger. Sauté meat for one minute, cover with water, add aniseed, cinnamon, and Chinese vegetable, and simmer until the meat is soft. Serve with plain boiled rice.

BARBECUED SPARE RIBS
SHIU PYE GWUT

3 lb. pork spare ribs
4 tablespoons honey
4 tablespoons vinegar
2 tablespoons sugar
4 tablespoons soy sauce

2 cloves garlic, crushed
A piece of green ginger, crushed
1 cup stock
1 tablespoon sherry

Mix together in a bowl the honey, vinegar, sugar, soy sauce, garlic, ginger, stock, and sherry. Chop spare ribs into 1½-inch lengths and marinate in mixture. (This can be kept in the refrigerator overnight.) Remove from marinade and roast in a moderate oven for one hour, basting occasionally. When cooked they should be crisp, but not dry.

BARBECUED PORK
CHAR SUI

1 lb. pork fillets
2 teaspoons sugar
Salt
2 teaspoons honey
3 teaspoons soy sauce, thick

2 tablespoons oil
1 teaspoon Chinese spice and/
or Chinese barbecue sauce
(hoy sin jeung)

Combine sugar, salt, honey, soy sauce, oil and Chinese spice and/or Chinese barbecue sauce in a bowl. (If using Chinese spice and barbecue sauce, omit honey.) Brush over pork fillets and let stand for one to two hours. Place on tripod in baking dish and roast for 10 minutes in a hot oven, then for 15 to 20 minutes in moderate heat, or cook over charcoal fire.

RED ROAST PORK WITH BEAN SPROUTS
CHAR SUI CHOW NGAR CHOY

1 lb. red roast pork (char sui)

Oil

A piece of green ginger, shredded

Salt

½ lb. bean sprouts

1 tablespoon sugar

1 tablespoon water

Heat pan, add a little oil, shredded green ginger, and salt, and when hot put in bean sprouts. Sprinkle with sugar and water and cook for one minute. Slice pork and mix together with bean sprouts, cooking for another minute.

LION'S HEAD
SEE JEE TOW

This is a New Year's Eve special dish, made to resemble the lion dancers in the Dragon Dance.

1 lb. pork

6 dried mushrooms

10 water chestnuts

1 onion

2 tablespoons soy sauce

Salt and pepper

1 tablespoon sugar

1 tablespoon sherry

½ teaspoon monosodium glutamate

1 egg

Oil for deep-frying

1 Chinese vegetable (gai larn)

½ cup water

1½ cups stock

Prepare mushrooms by soaking in hot water for 20 minutes. Mince together pork, chestnuts, onion, and mushrooms, and season with soy sauce, salt, pepper, sugar, sherry, and monosodium glutamate. Bind with egg and form into four meat balls about 2 inches thick. Heat pan, add oil, and deep-fry the balls until brown. Remove. Cut Chinese vegetable into lengths and sauté in a little oil for one minute, pour in water, simmer for one minute. Put the "lion's head" on top of the vegetable, add stock, and simmer for about 15 minutes.

CURRIED FLANK STEAK
GAR LEE BARR NARM

1 lb. flank steak (with sheet of sinew left on the side)	1 tablespoon curry powder
Salt and pepper	2 tablespoons curry paste
1 tablespoon soy sauce	A piece of green ginger, crushed
1 onion	2 cups water
2 yams or potatoes	1 tablespoon cornflour
Oil	1 cup coconut milk

Cut steak into one-inch cubes. Sprinkle with salt, pepper, and soy sauce. Peel onion and potatoes and cut into same size pieces. Heat pan, add oil, and sauté onion until soft. Add a little more oil if necessary, and sauté steak until it turns colour, then mix in curry powder and/or curry paste and cook for one minute. Add potatoes, green ginger, and water and simmer until potatoes are soft, adding more water if required. Thicken with blended cornflour and coconut milk (made by pouring boiling water on desiccated coconut), cooking a further couple of minutes. Serve with boiled rice and the usual side dishes. Suggestions: toasted coconut, chutney, pickled cucumbers, bananas and raisins, fried onion rings.

Hot chilli dip sauce: Shred 6 hot red and green chillies. Mix in ½ teaspoon salt, 2 teaspoons white vinegar, and 1 tablespoon vegetable oil.

4

Vegetables

THE CHINESE long ago discovered the secret of cooking vegetables so as to keep their colour and crispness and give them a pleasing taste. Contrary to the belief held by some people that vegetables cooked in the Chinese way are half done, they are in fact just done. Soft vegetables such as lettuce, Chinese spinach, mustard top, cabbage, watercress, and bean sprouts are allowed to cook in little or no water at all, because quick cooking in a hot pan brings out the natural juices. Hard vegetables such as broccoli, green beans, carrots, snow peas, bamboo shoots, lotus root, cauliflower can be parboiled before being mixed with meat or fish to be combined into a Chinese dish. If preparing for a dinner party, having the vegetables ready in this way means that it will take only a few minutes to combine all ingredients together, and the water used for cooking the vegetables can be used for sauces and gravies.

A number of Chinese vegetables that may be unfamiliar on the Western table are slowly making their appearance on the market; these include bean sprouts, water chestnuts, edible pea pods, bamboo shoots, lotus root, yams, gourds, melons both bitter and sweet, wong ah bark, mustard cabbage, Chinese parsley, chrysanthemum cabbage, and many types of Chinese spinach from that with soft pale-green leaves to that with firmer darker green leaves, all of which will bring a distinctive taste to your dish, as well as adding an oriental touch.

The Chinese make provision for periodical scarcity of

fresh vegetables by preserving when plentiful, and so can call upon a large variety of salted, dried, and pickled ingredients.

Bean sprouts can be cultivated in the kitchen by sprinkling green beans with warm water and putting them in a covered container overnight. Next morning, sprinkle with water again and keep covered with a damp hessian bag till the beans begin to sprout—which takes about two days. Keep the sprouted beans moist and in five days they should be about two inches long and ready for use. They are tender and crisp, and can be included in many Chinese dishes with great success, and are an added delight in a Chinese salad bowl. The soy bean can also be sprouted, but usually the sprout is tougher.

Flower petals, stalks, and even seeds are preserved and used as food, and gum jum, the dried stalks of the lotus plant, is ideal for serving with steamed chicken.

CHINESE SALAD DRESSING
SALAT JUP

3 tablespoons vegetable or salad oil
1 tablespoon vinegar
1 teaspoon soy sauce

1 teaspoon sugar
¼ teaspoon mustard
1 clove garlic, crushed

Mix or shake all ingredients together, and use with green salads as desired.

CANTONESE SALAD BOWL
KWANDUNG LARNG POON DIP

½ lb. bean sprouts
1 lettuce
A few slices red ginger pickles (hoong geung)

½ cup melon shred (gwah ying), or cucumber
¾ cup chopped celery
10 lychees

Cantonese Salad Bowl—*Continued*.

The bean sprouts are washed and steamed gently for about 2 minutes and allowed to become cold. Arrange all ingredients attractively in individual lettuce cups or on a bed of lettuce leaves. Serve with Chinese salad dressing. Sliced prawns, chicken, or red roast pork may be added if desired.

CRAB SALAD WITH SWEET-SOUR PICKLES
SIN TIM HAI SALAT

1 lettuce	$\frac{1}{2}$ lb. crabmeat
1 cup assorted sweet-sour pickles	2 hard-boiled eggs
	Chinese parsley

Wash lettuce, separate leaves and line a salad bowl with them. Arrange crabmeat, drained pickles, and egg slices in the leaves to form a decorative pattern. Garnish with Chinese parsley. Serve with Chinese salad dressing.

MANDARIN SALAD BOWL
BUKIN LARNG POON DIP

$\frac{1}{2}$ lb. bean sprouts, steamed	8 pickled leeks (sin tow)
2 tablespoons green melon shred (cheng gwah shee)	Lettuce
	Chinese parsley
2 white onions, peeled and cut into rings	Sesame seeds, toasted

Combine cold bean sprouts, melon shred, onions, and pickled leeks. Pile into lettuce cups, decorate with Chinese parsley, sprinkle with sesame seeds, and serve immediately. Can be used as a side salad or with cold meats. Alternatively the bean sprouts may be tossed in Chinese salad dressing before they are placed in lettuce cups.

FASTING FOOD
JIE

6 dried oysters (hor see)
6 mushrooms
3 sticks bean curd (foo jook)
A small portion of cellophane
  noodles (jun see)
1 cup snow peas (hor lan
  dow)

Oil
4 blocks bean curds (taofu)
½ teaspoon monosodium
  glutamate
2 tablespoons oyster sauce
Cornflour
Sesame seeds

Soak oysters overnight. Prepare mushrooms by soaking for 20 minutes in hot water, bean curd for 15 minutes, and cellophane noodles for 10 minutes. Drain all ingredients. Cut tips off snow peas and parboil for one minute. Heat pan, add oil, then sauté ingredients in this order: bean curds, oysters, foo jook, noodles, and snow peas. Add monosodium glutamate. Mix oyster sauce with cornflour and water, stir in and cook a further minute or two. Sprinkle with toasted sesame seeds. Serve hot.

This dish is eaten during the Moon Festival and on the second day of the New Year.

CELLOPHANE NOODLES
WITH CRAB
JUN SEE HAI

A small bundle of cellophane
  noodles (jun see)
6 mushrooms
10 water chestnuts
2 slices ham
1 small melon (jit gwah)
4 eggs
Salt
Oil

1 teaspoon sugar
1 tablespoon sherry
1 tin crab
½ teaspoon monosodium
  glutamate
1 teaspoon cornflour
2 tablespoons soy sauce
3 tablespoons stock

Soak cellophane noodles for 10 minutes in hot water. Remove, place in a deep pan, cover with cold water, and boil for 5 minutes. Drain. Prepare mushrooms by soaking in hot

Cellophane Noodles with Crab—*Continued.*

water for 20 minutes then shred together with chestnuts, ham, and melon. Beat eggs and salt together. Heat pan, add oil, and fry beaten eggs into a thin omelette. Cool and shred. Add more oil to pan and sauté mushrooms, season with sugar and sherry, add melon, chestnuts, cellophane noodles, ham, crab, and monosodium glutamate. Make sauce with cornflour, soy sauce, and stock, and add to mixture, stirring well together. Season. Cook for a further 2 minutes. Serve with a dip sauce made of soy sauce and sesame oil.

STEAMED BEAN SPROUTS
NGAR CHOY

Place prepared bean sprouts in a colander and steam over boiling water for 2 minutes. They are then ready to use with other recipes or to be included in a salad bowl when cool.

UPSIDE-DOWN MUSHROOMS
FUN JIN TOW DOONG GWOO

15 medium-sized mushrooms	2 tablespoons soy sauce
Oil	Salt and pepper
1 teaspoon sugar	Cornflour
1 tablespoon sherry	2 eggs
¼ lb. minced pork	2 tablespoons stock
½ cup minced prawns, un-cooked	1 teaspoon vegetable or sesame oil

Prepare mushrooms by soaking them in hot water for 20 minutes. Sauté in a little oil, add sugar and sherry, then arrange on a shallow plate, with the stems upwards. Mix pork and prawns together, season with soy sauce, salt, and pepper, then sprinkle with cornflour to bind lightly. Pack mixture on to mushrooms. Beat eggs and pour over mushrooms, then pour oil and stock over. Steam for about 40 minutes. **Garnish with Chinese parsley.**

STUFFED CUCUMBERS
YEUNG WONG GWAH

$\frac{1}{2}$ lb. minced meat
1 large onion, minced
2 tablespoons soy sauce
1 teaspoon sugar
Salt and pepper

1 teaspoon cornflour
2 medium-sized cucumbers
Oil
1 clove garlic, crushed
1 tablespoon stock

Place meat, onion, soy sauce, sugar, salt, and pepper in a bowl. Mix in cornflour and let stand 10 minutes. Peel most of the green skin off the cucumber, leaving on a few strips for decoration. Cut into lengths of about $1\frac{1}{2}$ inches and scoop out seeds. Pack filling into cucumber firmly. Heat pan, add oil, garlic, and a pinch of salt. Brown each side of filling, pour over stock, and simmer with lid on for 10 minutes, adding more liquid if necessary. If served with a sauce, remove cucumbers to a platter, add blended cornflour to pan juices, season, and cook for $1\frac{1}{2}$ minutes. When cold this can be used as a hors-d'oeuvre.

PICKLED CUCUMBERS
YIP WONG GWAH

Peel cucumber, leaving on strips of green skin for colour interest. Cut in half lengthwise and scoop out seeds. Slice finely crosswise and place in a bowl. Marinate in 2 teaspoons salt, 6 tablespoons sugar, 6 tablespoons vinegar, and 4 tablespoons water for 15 minutes. Squeeze out cucumber. Use liquor blended with cornflour, tomato paste, and soy sauce to make a sauce suitable for any sweet-sour recipe.

This is an excellent combination for sweet-sour spare ribs.

5

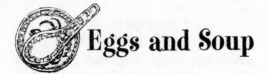

Eggs and Soup

EVERYONE has heard of "thousand-year-old" eggs, but in reality these eggs are only a few months old. Usually duck eggs are covered with a mixture of ashes, tea, lime, and salt, rolled in dried rice husks, and then buried for about four months. After this time, when they are ready to eat, the covers are broken off and the eggs are shelled. The yolks are an orange-green colour, with the albumen solidified like a dark green jelly with white star streaks. Thousand-year-old eggs are eaten with vinegar and ginger pickles, served as an appetizer, and have a taste so individual as to excite any palate.

In Chinese cookery, eggs are used to more advantage than just as a breakfast dish. Combined with seafood, poultry, pork, meats or vegetables, they make such favourites as egg foo yoong (omelettes) and steamed egg. Apart from the ordinary usage in cakes, custards, or just boiled in tea leaves, they are put into soups, and when made into a thin pancake and cut into very fine strips are used as a garnish for fried rice, noodle, or other dishes.

Hen and duck eggs are also preserved by salting, and these are ready for use in five to six weeks. They are hard boiled, cut into segments, have hot vegetable oil poured over them, and are served with plain boiled rice.

Apart from the delicate bird's nest soup and the incomparable shark fin soup, which are Feast Day fare, soups usually take very little time to prepare, providing there is a rich stock on hand. They are generally on the clear side,

Pork and Celery (Jee Yuk Chow Wun Yee), a nourishing dish to combine perfectly with a simple fried rice.

Lobster Omelette (Dai Har Foo Yoong). Several small omelettes may be preferred.

with chunks of meat and vegetables added, and there is always at least one bowl of soup in a simple meal. This type of soup is an ideal base for a combination of vegetables and the many dried ingredients that make an oriental soup.

There are special ingredients for soups intended for body-building during, for instance, a pregnancy, or after an illness, and medicinal herbs are added also, to help enrich the bloodstream. When a new baby is one month old (the Chinese consider that any time up to one month is a danger period for the baby), there is a celebration at which is served the speciality for this occasion—a soup made with whole chicken, fresh green ginger, and large pieces of fungi, simmered in rice wine. It is delicious.

BROWN STOCK
KNO YUK TONG

Meat bones
Soup meat
$\frac{1}{2}$ brown onion
Peppercorns

Water
Vegetables (celery, carrot, white beets, onion)

Brown the bones, soup meat, and half-onion under the griller or in the oven. Place in a large pot, cover with water, put in peppercorns, and bring to a boil. Simmer for $1\frac{1}{2}$ to 2 hours. Add vegetables and simmer further for another hour. Carefully remove scum and fat and strain through cloth. Bring to a boil, and when cool store in the refrigerator. (To be used for the base of sauces, gravies, and soups.)

CHICKEN STOCK
GAI TONG

Chicken carcass
Pieces of pork and pork bones
2 teaspoons soy sauce
Peppercorns

A piece of fresh green ginger
Vegetables (white onion, turnips, celery, carrot)

Place chicken carcass, pork, pork bones, soy sauce, peppercorns, and green ginger in a large pot with cold water to

D

Chicken Stock—*Continued.*

cover. Bring to a boil and simmer for 1½ to 2 hours. Put in roughly chopped vegetables and simmer for a further hour. Remove any scum and fat. Strain carefully. (It is not necessary to season this stock, for it is used as the base for other recipes, where they will be then seasoned.)

FISH STOCK
YEE TONG

Fish heads and trimmings
Celery
White onion
Turnips

Peppercorns
A two-inch piece of green ginger

Wash fish heads and trimmings thoroughly. Cover with water, add vegetables, peppercorns and ginger and bring to a boil. Continue to simmer for approximately one hour. Strain carefully and allow to cool.

CUCUMBER SOUP
GWAH TONG

½ cup dried shrimps (har mei)
6 mushrooms
2 medium-sized cucumbers
¼ lb. cooked ham
8 cups well-flavoured chicken
  stock

1 tablespoon soy sauce
Salt
1 inch green ginger
1 teaspoon monosodium
  glutamate
2 tablespoons sherry

Soak shrimps overnight. Prepare mushrooms by soaking in hot water for 20 minutes, and cut into strips. Peel cucumber, leaving a fine green strip of skin. Scoop out seeds with a spoon, cut lengthwise, and slice across. Chop cooked ham finely. Put stock, soy sauce, salt, and ginger in a saucepan, bring to a boil, add mushrooms and shrimps. Simmer for 30 minutes. Add cucumber and cook for a further 5 minutes. Season with monosodium glutamate, and before serving sprinkle chopped ham on top.

Cooked shrimps may be used instead of dried.

SCALLOP SOUP
GONG YO GEE TONG

¼ lb. dried scallops
1 quart well-flavoured
   chicken stock

2 eggs
Shallots, chopped
Salt and pepper

Soak scallops overnight. Shred them (they will fall away easily) and add to chicken stock. Bring to a boil and simmer for 30 minutes. Before serving beat in eggs, add chopped shallots, and salt and pepper to taste.

EGG FLOWER SOUP
FAR DARN TONG

1 quart chicken stock
½ teaspoon monosodium
   glutamate

Salt and pepper
2 eggs
1 tablespoon chopped shallots

Into boiling rich chicken stock add monosodium glutamate. Season with salt and pepper and simmer for 10 minutes. Beat eggs together in a bowl and pour into stock. Stir well until eggs begin to cook and spread out like a flower. Serve garnished with chopped shallots.

SWEET CORN SOUP
SOOK MAI TONG

1 tin whole kernel corn
½ lb. shin beef
Salt
1 teaspoon soy sauce
2 teaspoons oil or lard

A piece of green ginger
8 cups brown stock
1 egg
1 teaspoon monosodium glutamate

Cut meat into chunks, season with salt and soy sauce. Heat pan, add oil and crushed ginger, and when hot sauté meat for 2 minutes. Pour in stock and bring to a boil. Simmer until meat is soft and then add sweet corn and simmer a further 5 minutes. Remove meat pieces, pour in beaten egg, then monosodium glutamate, and stir well. Serve garnished with chopped shallots.

PORK BALL SOUP
JEE YUK YIN TONG

1 lb. pork mince	1 quart stock
Salt	1 bunch Chinese spinach
1 tablespoon soy sauce	½ teaspoon monosodium
1 egg yolk	glutamate

Mix pork with salt, soy sauce, and beaten egg yolk. Shape into small balls about one inch in diameter. Bring stock to a boil, drop in pork balls, and simmer for 15 minutes. Cut spinach into pieces and add to soup, cooking a further 5 minutes. Season with salt and monosodium glutamate. Serve in a deep bowl accompanied by a dip sauce of oyster sauce and sesame oil.

ASPARAGUS SOUP
LO SOON TONG

1 quart chicken stock	Green shallots, chopped
1 cup shredded cooked	½ teaspoon monosodium
chicken	glutamate
1 tin asparagus pieces	Salt

Bring chicken stock to a boil, add shredded chicken, asparagus pieces and liquor, and simmer for 5 minutes. Before serving, add shallots, monosodium glutamate, and salt to taste.

STEAMED EGG
JENG DARN

¼ lb. minced pork or veal	2 tablespoons milk
Salt	1 teaspoon vegetable oil
2 teaspoons soy sauce	1 teaspoon sesame oil
Oil	Green ends of shallots,
3 eggs	chopped

Season meat with salt and soy sauce and sauté it in a little oil until it turns colour. Beat egg yolks and add to meat with salt to taste. Fold in lightly beaten egg whites and

Steamed Egg—*Continued.*

milk. Spoon mixture into a deep bowl, pour on sesame oil, vegetable oil, and chopped green shallots. Cover with greaseproof paper, place over boiling water in a steamer and steam for 20 to 25 minutes. Turn out and serve. Garnish with Chinese parsley (this is similar to the parsley sold by most greengrocers but the leaves are finer and the taste more delicate).

PLAIN FRIED EGGS
JIN DARN

Eggs	Soy sauce
Oil	Sesame oil
Shallots, chopped	

Heat pan, add a little oil, and when hot break in each egg separately. When the egg starts to set, sprinkle the yolk with chopped shallots. Remove to a warm plate. Pour over each egg ½ teaspoon soy sauce and ½ teaspoon sesame oil. Serve with plain boiled rice.

CRAB OMELETTE
FOO YOONG HAI

4 or 5 eggs	Oil
2 teaspoons soy sauce	½ cup water or stock
Salt	1 teaspoon cornflour
½ lb. tin crabmeat	1 teaspoon oyster sauce
¼ lb. bean sprouts	1 teaspoon sherry

Beat eggs in a large bowl. Add 1 teaspoon of the soy sauce, salt to flavour, and flaked crabmeat. Mix well. Remove tips of bean sprouts. Heat pan, add oil, and sauté bean sprouts for one minute. Remove. Add to egg mixture when cold. Add more oil to the pan, and take about 2 tablespoons of the mixture and make into small omelettes, browning on both sides, or folding over.

Crab Omelette—*Continued.*

For the sauce, boil water or stock with cornflour blended with the oyster sauce. Add remaining teaspoon of soy sauce, then the sherry. Simmer until thick. Pour this sauce over the omelettes and garnish with Chinese parsley.

RICE OMELETTE
FOO YOONG FARN

4 eggs	Oil
Salt	1 tablespoon cornflour
Shallots, chopped	$\frac{1}{4}$ cup water
1 cup cold cooked rice	$\frac{1}{2}$ cup stock
2 tablespoons olive nuts or	1 tablespoon sherry
almonds	2 teaspoons oyster sauce, thin

Beat eggs, salt to taste, and chopped shallots together. Add rice and nuts (almonds should be shredded). Heat pan, add oil and pour in mixture. When set, fold and brown on other side. Turn on to a warm plate.

For the sauce, mix cornflour with water, add stock, sherry, and oyster sauce and bring to a boil. Simmer for one minute. Pour sauce over omelette and serve hot.

SALTED DUCK EGGS
HARM DARN

12 duck eggs	1 cup coarse salt
1 quart water	

Bring water and salt to the boil. Cool. Place eggs into the salted water which has been put into an earthenware pot or glass jar with screw top. Set aside in a cool place for 6 weeks. When ready for use, cover the egg with cold water, bring to a boil, and cook for 10 minutes. Cut in halves through the shell, take a spoon and scoop out the egg and cut it into wedges. Serve with sesame oil, as an appetizer.

CHINESE OMELETTE
FOO YOONG

4 eggs
Salt and white pepper
½ teaspoon soy sauce
½ oz. clarified butter or 1
tablespoon oil

½ cup flaked cooked crab
2 tablespoons cooked shredded mushrooms
A few chopped green shallots

Beat eggs together and season with salt, pepper, and soy sauce. Heat pan, add butter or oil, and when butter is foaming (if using oil, it should be hot) pour in eggs, stir briskly with fork and then put in crab, mushrooms, and shallots quickly. Fold over, allow the outside to colour, and turn out on a warm serving plate. Rub a piece of butter quickly across the surface to make the omelette glossy. Serve with lemon wedges and extra whole mushrooms for a garnish.

PRAWN OMELETTE
FOO YOONG HAR

2 cups bean sprouts
6 eggs
2 tablespoons water
1 tablespoon soy sauce
½ teaspoon monosodium
glutamate

Salt and pepper
½ lb. raw shelled prawns
Oil
One inch of green ginger,
shredded
1 medium-sized onion

Cut off both tips of bean sprouts, wash, and blanch for one minute. Beat eggs with water, soy sauce, salt, pepper, and monosodium glutamate. Clean and slice prawns, then sauté in oil, with shredded ginger, until they turn pink. Remove. Slice onion and sauté until soft. Return prawns, add bean sprouts, and more oil if necessary. Cook for a further minute. Pour egg over mixture, and when set fold into an omelette. This can be cooked as one large omelette or several smaller ones.

SMALL OMELETTES
FOO YOONG JAY

$\frac{1}{2}$ lb. pork   6 eggs
Shallots   Oil
1 tablespoon soy sauce   1 tablespoon sherry
1 teaspoon sugar   2 teaspoons oyster sauce
Salt and pepper $\frac{3}{4}$ cup stock

Mince pork and shallots together and season with soy sauce, sugar, salt, and pepper. Beat eggs together. Heat pan, add oil, and when hot drop in about 1 tablespoon of egg, then immediately put in 2 teaspoons pork mixture. Fold, brown one side, then turn over and brown the other. Remove. Serve with oyster sauce and garnish with Chinese parsley.

 **Poultry**

IT IS INTERESTING to note that the Chinese serve poultry with the bone intact. No first-class meal would be complete without at least one chicken dish, and it is permissible to serve chicken more than one way in the same menu. In fact, the prestige of the Chinese chef is measured by his ability to make innumerable chicken dishes without repeating the flavour. A favourite method is to place a young chicken in boiling water for a few minutes until it is barely done, and then serve it with a variety of dip sauces.

No part of the chicken is wasted. Everything is used—skin, wing, aileron, head, feet, liver, gizzard, and even the blood. Usually the chicken is served cut into bite-size pieces, cut through the bone with a cleaver, and arranged back in place on the platter.

Cantonese ducks are famous the world over, and the salted preserved ducks are extremely popular as an appetizer. Peking Duck is a luxury dish, and a whole course can be arranged with the duck made into various dishes. In this instance, the skin is of particular importance, for it is cooked and served as a dish on its own, being very crisp and tasty. It is eaten with a fruit chutney and a hot bread roll or pancake with the crisp skin in the centre, folded like a sandwich.

LYCHEE CHICKEN
LICHEE GAI

1 chicken, about 3 lb.	1 tablespoon sherry
12 water chestnuts	1 egg white
1 onion	Oil for deep-frying
3 tablespoons cornflour	1 large tin lychees
3 tablespoons soy sauce	2 tablespoons stock
Salt	¾ cup lychee juice

Lychees are a fruit with white flesh and a large seed, encased in a red flexible mottled skin. They are very luscious and juicy. To prepare lychee chicken, fillet the chicken and chop together finely with water chestnuts and onion. Place in a bowl and mix in 2 tablespoons of the cornflour, 2 tablespoons of the soy sauce, salt, sherry, and egg white. Form into small balls about 1½ inches in diameter, heat oil, and deep-fry until brown. Drain, and arrange on a platter and garnish with lychees. Serve with lychee sauce. To make the sauce, mix the remaining tablespoon of soy sauce with the cornflour, stock, and lychee juice. Heat until boiled, stirring constantly.

CHICKEN WITH CAPSICUMS
LAIT JEW GAI

1 young chicken	3 or 4 capsicums or hot
Salt	chillies
1 tablespoon cornflour	¾ cup chicken stock
2 tablespoons soy sauce	1 tablespoon white wine
Oil	1 teaspoon cornflour (for
1 onion	sauce)

Fillet the chicken and cut into one-inch cubes. Sprinkle with salt, cornflour, and soy sauce and allow it to stand for 15 minutes. Deep-fry in hot oil until it turns colour. Remove and drain. Slice onion and capsicums the same size as the chicken pieces. Remove excess oil from pan, leaving enough to sauté onion until soft, then capsicums. Return chicken to the vegetables, pour in stock and wine, and

Chicken with Capsicums—*Continued.*

thicken with blended cornflour, cooking for a further minute or two.

MANDARIN CHICKEN AND VEGETABLES
GAI KOW CHOY TOW

1 small chicken	1 onion
½ lb. chicken giblets	½ cup green beans
2 tablespoons soy sauce	2 stalks Chinese vegetable
Salt	(wong ah bark)
1 tablespoon sherry	¼ cup green peas
2 tablespoons cornflour	2 stalks celery
Oil	1 tablespoon chopped shallots
1 clove garlic	1¾ cups stock
1 inch green ginger, shredded	1 teaspoon sesame oil

Clean and cut chicken and giblets into small pieces. Season with soy sauce, salt, and sherry and mix in 1 tablespoon of the cornflour. Prepare vegetables by cutting into pieces of a similar size to the chicken pieces. Heat pan, add oil, crushed garlic and shredded ginger. Sauté vegetables in this order: onion, beans, cabbage, peas, celery, and shallots. Add stock. Cook for a further minute. Remove and place aside. Clean pan, heat, add oil, then sauté chicken and giblets. When they turn colour, return the vegetables with liquor, turning over frequently, and thicken with blended cornflour, if necessary. Before serving, pour over sesame oil.

POT ROAST CHICKEN AND MUSHROOMS
WAT GAI DOONG GWOO

1 young chicken, about 3 lb.	A piece of green ginger, light-
12 dried mushrooms	ly crushed
4 tablespoons soy sauce	3 or 4 tablespoons oil
1 teaspoon five-spice (heung	1 cup water
lo fun)	Chopped lengths of shallots
1 tablespoon sherry	

Pot Roast Chicken and Mushrooms—*Continued*.

Salt cleaned chicken lightly inside and outside. Prepare mushrooms by soaking in hot water for 20 minutes. Combine soy sauce, five-spice, and sherry in a bowl. Dip the piece of ginger into the sauce and wipe all over the chicken flesh with it. If possible, let it stand for 20 minutes. Heat pot, add oil, and cook chicken all over until nicely browned. Add mushrooms, water, and cook one minute, then cover with lid and begin to steam. After 15 minutes, place mushrooms inside chicken and continue steaming until tender. Add a little more liquid if required. Before serving, add shallots. Garnish with fried prawn crisps (har beang).

If you prefer a thicker sauce, blend the liquor from the chicken with cornflour and serve the chicken cut up with the bone, place on a platter, surround with prawn crisps, and pour sauce over chicken.

CHICKEN DE CHENE AND MUSHROOMS
DOONG GWOO CLEAM JUP

1 whole chicken, about 3 lb.	2 tablespoons margarine
Salt	3 tablespoons plain flour
A piece of green ginger	Chicken stock
10 dried mushrooms	2 tablespoons sherry
1 teaspoon monosodium glutamate	$\frac{1}{2}$ cup cream

Wash and clean the chicken and rub with salt inside and outside. Place in a large pot with green ginger, mushrooms which have been prepared by soaking in hot water for 20 minutes, add monosodium glutamate and water to cover. Bring to a boil, and simmer till tender (about one hour). Drain and allow to cool. Remove meat, and return bones to make chicken stock. Take out mushrooms and cut into $\frac{3}{4}$-inch dice, also the chicken meat. Melt margarine over

Chicken de Chene and Mushrooms—*Continued*.

slow heat, and gradually add the flour, making into a smooth paste. Gradually add hot chicken stock (which has been strained carefully to remove all fat) until the consistency of cream. Mix in chicken and mushrooms until heated, then sherry and cream. Sprinkle with chopped shallots.

CHICKEN AND ALMONDS
HUNG YUN GAI

1 lb. chicken meat	$\frac{1}{2}$ teaspoon monosodium
Salt	glutamate
A pinch of bicarbonate soda	1 onion
1 tablespoon cornflour	1 cup prepared mushrooms
1 egg white	$\frac{1}{2}$ cup diced green beans
1 teaspoon sesame oil	$\frac{1}{2}$ cup diced celery
1 tablespoon white wine	$\frac{3}{4}$ cup diced water chestnuts
Oil for deep-frying	Toasted almonds

Cut the chicken meat into small dice and mix with salt, soda, cornflour, egg white, sesame oil, wine, and monosodium glutamate. Dice all vegetables into a similar size. Heat pan and add enough oil to deep-fry chicken until it is just coloured. Remove and drain. Take out most of the oil and sauté the vegetables in this order: onion, mushroom, beans, celery, and chestnuts. Add a little water to soften if required. Season. Return chicken and mix well together. Bind together with a sauce made with 1 tablespoon soy sauce, 1 tablespoon cornflour, 1 cup chicken stock, and cook for a further 2 or 3 minutes. Sprinkle with toasted almonds before serving. Surround with a garnish of cellophane noodles.

The white meat of the chicken (breast for preference) makes the authentic dish of Chicken and Almonds, but for economy every part of the flesh may be used.

VELVET CHICKEN
YOONG YUEN GAI

4 chicken breasts	$\frac{1}{4}$ lb. lard
$\frac{1}{2}$ cup water	1 inch green ginger, finely
2 teaspoons cornflour	sliced
Salt	1 cup chicken stock
$\frac{1}{2}$ teaspoon monosodium	2 teaspoons sherry
glutamate	1 tablespoon lotus powder
5 egg whites	Shredded cooked ham

Slice chicken in thin fillets, removing tendon. Chop and pound with back of a cleaver or a heavy knife, adding a little water if too dry. Sprinkle with cornflour, salt, monosodium glutamate, pound again, and brush with one of the egg whites. Slowly add remainder of water, working in well. Beat the other 4 egg whites and slowly stir in the chicken mixture, transferring to a bowl if preferred. Heat pan, melt lard and immediately put in chicken mixture, stirring vigorously. Drain the lard from the mixture through a strainer. Heat pan again, add a little lard and ginger, and when hot put in 1 tablespoon of the mixture at a time and cook quickly on both sides. Remove and drain.

Any cooked vegetables may be added to this mixture before it is cooked. Some suggestions are mushrooms, snow peas, string beans, celery, Chinese greens.

To make the sauce, mix together stock, salt to taste, and sherry. Bring to a boil. Thicken with lotus powder and pour over chicken. Garnish with shredded cooked ham.

FRIED CHICKEN
JOW GAI

1 young chicken, about 3 lb.	1 clove garlic, crushed
$\frac{1}{2}$ cup soy sauce	2 inches green ginger, crushed
1 tablespoon sherry	2 eggs
1 tablespoon sugar	Breadcrumbs
Salt	Oil for deep-frying

Clean and cut chicken into large pieces and place in a bowl. Mix together soy sauce, sherry, sugar, salt, garlic, and gin-

Fried Chicken—*Continued.*

ger. Pour this over the chicken pieces and let it stand for 20 minutes. Beat eggs. Dip chicken pieces into egg, then into breadcrumbs, and deep-fry in hot oil. Drain.

LEMON CHICKEN
NING MOONG GAI

1 plump young chicken	2 lemons
Salt	3 tablespoons oil
2 tablespoons soy sauce	1 clove garlic
2 teaspoons sugar	1 inch green ginger
1 tablespoon sherry	1½ cups stock or water
½ teaspoon monosodium glutamate	Chinese parsley

Clean, wash and dry chicken. Rub inside and out with salt. Mix soy sauce, sugar, sherry, monosodium glutamate, and lemon juice together. Heat saucepan, add oil, garlic, and ginger. Brown chicken in this, then add stock or water and simmer until soft. Remove from saucepan and cut into segments. Garnish with Chinese parsley and serve with lemon wedges.

PINEAPPLE CHICKEN
BOR LOR GAI

1 young chicken, 2 to 3 lb.	1 clove garlic
½ cup soy sauce	4 tablespoons pineapple juice
Salt	¾ cup water
2 inches green ginger	Pineapple pieces
2 teaspoons sugar	Cornflour
1 tablespoon sherry	Chinese parsley
3 tablespoons oil	

Clean and wash chicken. Mix together soy sauce, salt, ginger, sugar, and sherry. Rub over chicken and let it stand for 20 minutes. Heat a deep pan, add oil and garlic, and brown the chicken on both sides. Add remaining soy sauce liquid, pineapple juice, and the water, and simmer until soft. Cut chicken into segments and arrange on a platter with pieces

Pineapple Chicken—*Continued.*

of pineapple. Pour liquid over chicken, thickened as required with blended cornflour. Garnish with Chinese parsley and serve.

CHICKEN WINGS
GAI YICK

1 lb. chicken wings, cut in halves
4 hard-boiled eggs, shelled
3 tablespoons sugar
½ cup soy sauce
1 petal dried aniseed (bark gock)
1 cup water
2 teaspoons five-spice (heung lo fun)
2 teaspoons cornflour
1 tablespoon sherry
1 inch green ginger, crushed
2 tablespoons oil

Mix all ingredients together except chicken wings and eggs, bring to a boil, then add chicken wings and simmer for 15 minutes. Add whole eggs and simmer for another 20 minutes. Serve as individual hors-d'oeuvres.

An alternative method is to season the wings with soy sauce and salt and deep-fry until lightly browned, then continue as above.

CHICKEN WITH BEAN SPROUTS
GAI CHOW NGAR CHOY

1 chicken, 2 to 3 lb.
Salt
2 tablespoons soy sauce
1 tablespoon cornflour
2 tablespoons oil
1 clove garlic
1 inch green ginger, crushed
2½ cups bean sprouts
1 tablespoon sugar
1 cup chicken stock
1 tablespoon mushroom sauce

Fillet chicken and cut into slices. Season with salt, soy sauce, and cornflour. Heat pan, add oil, garlic, and ginger, and sauté chicken until it turns colour. Remove. Wash and remove root tip from the bean sprouts. Drain off excess water. Heat the pan, add oil and salt, and sauté bean sprouts with sugar for about one minute. Return chicken

Chicken with Bean Sprouts—*Continued*.

to bean sprouts, mixing well together, then pour in chicken stock, and simmer until tender. Thicken with blended cornflour and mushroom sauce, cooking a further minute. Serve with ham fried rice. (Mushroom sauce is now available in small cans.)

STEAMED CHICKEN
JENG GAI

1 chicken, 2 to 3 lb. (or legs and wings of chicken)
Salt and pepper
2 tablespoons soy sauce
1 tablespoon sugar
1 tablespoon sherry
1 inch green ginger, shredded
1 cup lotus stems (gum jum)

6 to 8 dried mushrooms (doong gwoo)
4 or 5 red dates (hoong jow)
1 tablespoon vegetable oil
2 teaspoons sesame oil
3 tablespoons chicken stock
A few green shallots, chopped

Chop chicken into pieces without removing the bones. Season with salt, pepper, soy sauce, sugar, sherry, and ginger, and let marinate for 30 minutes. Wash lotus stems by soaking them in hot water, then squeeze dry. Soak mushrooms in hot water for 20 minutes together with red dates. Remove mushroom stems and slice. Cut red dates, removing seed. Have a deep bowl ready for steaming. Firstly put the lotus stems in, then chicken and its liquid, mushrooms, and red dates. Pour vegetable oil, sesame oil, and stock over, and steam for 20 minutes. Sprinkle with green shallots and serve from the bowl accompanied by plain boiled rice.

CHINESE CHAFING DISH
DAR BIN LOO

1 young chicken
1 tablespoon soy sauce
Salt
1 bundle cellophane noodles (jun see)

Chinese spinach, cut in 2-inch lengths
Boiled rice
6 eggs
Petals of white chrysanthemums

E

Chinese Chafing Dish—*Continued.*

This dish is better known as Chinese Sukiyaki. Instead of the young chicken, you may use 1 lb. fish fillets, chicken livers, or thinly sliced beef, or a combination of chicken and chicken livers. Slice chicken, meat, or fish very thinly (in pieces about 2 inches long). Cover carcass with chicken stock, water, and soy sauce. Bring to a boil. Add salt to taste, and simmer until a rich stock results. Soak half of cellophane noodles in water, and deep-fry the other half. Arrange ingredients on separate plates around the chafing dish in this order: meat, chicken or fish, cellophane noodles, raw eggs, chrysanthemum petals. Place half the hot stock in the chafing dish and invite each guest to cook his own portion of vegetable (2 minutes), then meat or fish (3 minutes). Add soft cellophane noodles to heat, break eggs into the chafing dish to poach, and sprinkle with chrysanthemum petals. When the eggs are cooked, let each guest fill his bowl with rice and add ingredients from the chafing dish, using fried noodles as a garnish.

If preferred, the eggs may be left raw and used as a dip for the various foods. Dip sauces served with this dish are soy sauce and sesame oil, hot chilli sauce with mustard, or oyster sauce and vegetable oil.

ROAST CHICKEN
SUI GAI

1 young chicken, about 3 lb.	½ cup oil
1 clove garlic, crushed	Salt
2 inches green ginger	2 teaspoons five-spice (heung
½ cup soy sauce	lo fun)
1 tablespoon sherry	Prawn crisps (har beang)

Clean, wash and dry chicken. Combine crushed garlic, ginger in one piece, soy sauce, sherry, oil, salt, and five-spice powder in a bowl. Take the piece of ginger, dip into sauce and rub it over the chicken, inside and out. Let chicken

Roast Chicken—*Continued.*

stand for 30 minutes, then roast in a moderate oven for about 1½ hours, basting with soy sauce mixture every 15 minutes until cooked. Cut chicken into segments and arrange on a platter with fried prawn crisps.

CURRIED CHICKEN
GAR LEE GAI

1 young chicken	2 tablespoons curry powder,
2 potatoes	or quantity to taste
2 onions	1 teaspoon curry paste
2 tablespoons oil	1½ cups water
1 clove garlic	Cornflour

Clean and chop chicken into 1½-inch pieces. Cut potatoes into pieces the same size. Peel onions and cut into sections of a similar size to the chicken. Heat pan, add oil and garlic, and sauté onion until soft. Add curry powder and paste, stir lightly for half a minute, then add potatoes and chicken. Sauté, mixing well so that curry coats these pieces. Add about 1½ cups water and simmer until the potatoes are cooked. Thicken with a roux and hot milk to make up one cup, and mix into curried chicken. Serve with boiled rice.

CHICKEN IN ASPIC
CHER LEE DOONG GAI

½ lb. chicken meat	2 cups water or consommé
2 teaspoons soy sauce	Chinese parsley
Salt	Lettuce
1 small piece agar-agar (sea-	Cucumber
weed)	

Cut chicken into small pieces and season with soy sauce and salt. Arrange in a small bowl and steam for 20 minutes. Soak agar-agar in the water or consommé for 10 minutes and then boil it for 15 minutes. Strain. Pour into a deep bowl and add the chicken pieces. Let cool in the refrigerator for 1 to 1½ hours, or until set. When ready to

Chicken in Aspic—*Continued*.

serve, place bowl in hot water long enough to ensure that
the aspic will leave the bowl, then turn onto a platter. Garnish with Chinese parsley, lettuce, and cucumber.

Dissolved gelatine may be used instead of agar-agar if desired.

CANTON DUCK
LARP ARP

Wipe clean a Canton duck, which is flat, with a damp cloth
and cut with a sharp cleaver into strips about 3 inches long.
Steam for 15 to 20 minutes. Garnish with Chinese parsley.

This is served as an appetizer, and eaten with hot boiled
rice. The duck sections may be placed on top of the rice
and steamed while it is cooking. One quarter of the duck
would be enough for two portions.

BRAISED DUCK WITH LILY BUDS
FAR JEE MUN ARP

1 duck	6 dried mushrooms
½ cup soy sauce	½ cup lily buds (far jee)
Salt and pepper	½ cup fungi (chee yee)
1 tablespoon sugar	A piece of bamboo shoot
½ cup sherry	Oil
2 inches green ginger, crushed	2 or 3 cups water or stock
1 clove garlic, crushed	

Combine soy sauce, salt, pepper, sugar, sherry, ginger, and
garlic in a bowl. Rub cleaned duck inside and out with
this mixture. Soak mushrooms in hot water for 20 minutes.
Slice. Soak lily buds and fungi in hot water for 10 minutes.
Drain. Heat pan, add oil, and fry fungi, mushrooms, sliced
bamboo shoots, and lily buds for a minute or two, with a
little water. Heat a large deep pan, add oil, and brown the
duck. Add mixture from other pan, water, and the soy
sauce liquor. Cover with a lid and simmer until very tender. Serve whole—each person breaking away his own
serving with chopsticks.

MINCED PIGEON
BARK GUP SOONG

2 pigeons	Oil
Lettuce	½ cup stock
1 large onion	1 tablespoon sugar
2 stalks celery	1 tablespoon soy sauce
4 dried mushrooms	1 teaspoon cornflour
A piece of bamboo shoot	

Clean and wash pigeons, remove all meat and mince it finely. Shred lettuce and place on a platter. Mince the vegetables. Heat pan, add oil, and sauté the pigeon meat for half a minute, then add vegetables, mixing well together and cooking for a further minute. Pour in stock, sugar, and soy sauce and thicken with blended cornflour. Simmer for another 2 minutes. Pour this mixture over the shredded lettuce and serve with plain boiled rice or toasted noodles.

STEAMED PIGEONS
DUN BARK GUP

2 pigeons	Soy sauce
4 oz. medicinal herbs (chun por loong)	Salt
	½ cup brandy

Clean and wash pigeons and put them whole into a steamer with the medicinal herbs, soy sauce, salt, and water to cover. Steam for 2 hours or until the meat is tender. Just before serving, pour in the brandy. Serve in separate bowls, placing in the meat, then the herbs, and pouring some of the liquor into each bowl. Each person also has a dip sauce made of soy sauce with hot vegetable oil and/or sesame oil added.

CHICKEN FRIED NOODLES
GAI CHOW MEIN

½ lb. fresh egg noodles
Oil for deep-frying
1½ cups cooked chicken
  shreds
1 egg
3 or 4 dried mushrooms
A piece of bamboo shoot
½ cup cooked ham
1 cup green beans

Salt and pepper
1 teaspoon sugar
1 tablespoon cornflour
1 cup chicken stock
1 tablespoon soy sauce
1 tablespoon sherry
½ teaspoon monosodium
  glutamate

Deep-fry noodles in hot oil until golden brown and crisp.
Drain on absorbent paper and arrange on a platter. Make
a very thin omelette with egg and shred when cool. Then
shred prepared mushrooms, bamboo shoot, ham, and
parboiled beans. Heat pan, add a little oil and sauté mushrooms with salt to taste and sugar. Mix in bamboo shoot,
ham, beans and chicken, turning over frequently. Bind
mixture with sauce and serve on top of fried noodles.
Sprinkle with shredded egg.

To make the sauce, blend 1 tablespoon cornflour with a
little warm water, add to stock and bring to a boil. Pour in
soy sauce, sherry, and monosodium glutamate, then add
salt to taste. Simmer for 2 or 3 minutes.

7

 Seafood

EAST differs from West in so many ways, and the serving of the fish dish is one of these instances, because in a Chinese banquet it is brought in towards the end of the meal, whereas in a westernized menu it is served at the beginning. But wherever the seafood is placed on the menu, the Chinese chef is a genius in its preparation; through long practice he has learnt to disguise the fishy taste by the judicious use of seasonings and pickled vegetables.

Fish should be cooked so that the flesh leaves the bone and is moist and not dried out by overcooking. A very successful way to achieve this texture is by steaming with fresh green ginger, seasonings, and a few slices of mushrooms—all that is needed, if the fish is fresh, for a delicious, subtly flavoured dish. The Chinese are very proud to boast that there is a different seafood for every day of the year, and this is not surprising when you think of the lengthy coastline of China, its rivers and lakes, not to mention the private pools where both fresh-water and salt-water fish are bred. Many families in China live on the fishing boats, earning their living as the result of the catch, and many of the poorer people subsist on rice and salt fish alone, which, surprisingly, makes a very appetizing meal.

Some of the bigger restaurants have a large indoor pool to keep the fish alive, and the customer can choose the fish desired and request the method of cooking on the spot. There are also "floating" ship restaurants where seafood is the speciality: huge tanks are anchored on the ship's side and the fish are there for the customer to choose from.

SHRIMP BALLS
HAR YIN JAY

1 lb. cleaned and shelled
  raw shrimps
Salt
1 egg white

Oil for deep-frying
2 teaspoons soy sauce
Black pepper

Chop shrimps till they make a fine mince. Season with salt.
Beat egg white until stiff, and thoroughly blend in the
shrimp mixture. Take 1 teaspoon of this at a time and drop
into hot oil. Brown evenly. Drain on absorbent paper.
Serve with a dip sauce made from soy sauce and black
pepper.

BUTTERFLY PRAWNS
WUCEP HAR

2 lb. raw prawns
Strips of bacon ½ inch by 2
  inches

Thin fritter batter
Cornflour
Oil for deep-frying

Wash, clean, and shell prawns, leaving on the tail-pieces.
Split each prawn in half as far as the tail and at this point
wind a strip of bacon round it, pushing a toothpick
through so that the bacon is caught in the centre of the
toothpick. Now bring one half of the prawn down and
catch the tip to one end of the toothpick. Do the same with
the other half. (The prawn now resembles a butterfly in
form.) Sprinkle with cornflour and dip into thin batter.
Deep-fry in hot oil until golden brown. Drain on absorbent
paper.

BASIC FISH MIXTURE
YEE BEANG

3 lb. whole fish
Salt and pepper
2 tablespoons soy sauce

1 dessertspoon sugar
2 tablespoons chopped shallots
Oil for deep-frying

Basic Fish Mixture—*Continued.*

A firm-fleshed fish should be used for this recipe, which is for a large quantity so that after being cooked some of it may be stored in the refrigerator for another meal. Wash the fish. Cut off fillets, leaving skin. Scrape flesh from underside with a spoon. Season with salt, pepper, soy sauce, and sugar. Add shallots. Into a small bowl put some water and dissolve 1 teaspoon salt. Damp the hand with this salt water and knead the fish mixture lightly. Fashion into balls, shape to desired size, and sprinkle with a little cornflour. Deep-fry in oil or lard until cooked. Drain.

When making large fish cakes with this basic mixture, add (if desired) dried mushrooms, first soaked and minced. Make into flat cakes about 3 inches in diameter and half an inch high.

FISH BALLS ORIENTAL
CHOW YEE YIN

Fish balls 1 inch in diameter	1 tablespoon sugar
1 tablespoon fungi (chee yee)	1 tablespoon cornflour
1 large onion	½ cup stock
3 or 4 stalks young celery	1 teaspoon sesame oil
Oil	Salt
1 clove garlic, crushed	A few green shallots, chopped
1 inch green ginger, crushed	

To make the fish balls see recipe for Basic Fish Mixture. Prepare fungi by soaking in warm water for 20 minutes, then wash, rinse, and drain. Peel and slice onion. Cut celery stalks in short lengths. Heat a little oil in a pan, add crushed garlic and ginger, and sauté onion for 1 minute. Add fungi, sugar, celery, and lastly the fish balls. Make a smooth paste with cornflour and water, add stock, sesame oil, and salt. Pour this into the mixture, cooking until it thickens. Garnish with chopped shallots. Serve with a dip sauce made of soy sauce, a little hot vegetable oil, and pepper to taste.

FISH CAKE WITH MELON SHRED
YEE BEANG GWAH SEE

3 fish cakes about 3 inches in diameter

1 small melon (jit gwah)

½ bunch stringless green beans (twao gock), or ½ lb. French beans

1 clove garlic, crushed

1 inch green ginger, crushed

Salt

1 tablespoon sugar

3 or 4 hot chillies (optional)

1 tablespoon cornflour

½ cup stock

A few cellophane noodles (jun see) deep-fried and crushed

Cut fish cakes in strips. (For recipe see page 60.) Peel melon, remove seeds, cut into enough shreds for 2 cups. Cut beans in lengths, blanch for one minute. Heat pan, add a little oil, and garlic and green ginger. Put in melon shreds, salt to taste, and sugar. Sauté until soft. Add beans, fish cake, and shredded chillies, and mix well together. Bind with cornflour and stock. Turn onto a platter and surround with cellophane noodles. Serve with a dip sauce of soy sauce, sesame oil and black pepper.

FISH-BALL SOUP
YEE YIN TONG

Fish balls 1 inch in diameter

4 cups stock

½ teaspoon monosodium glutamate

Salt

Green ends of shallots, chopped

Bring stock to a boil, add fish balls (see recipe on page 60), and simmer for 10 minutes. Add monosodium glutamate. When ready to serve, add salt to taste, and chopped shallots. Serve with a dip sauce made from soy sauce and/or chilli sauce.

SHRIMPS IN ASPIC
CHER LEE DOONG HAR

½ lb. raw shelled shrimps
1 inch green ginger, shredded
1 tablespoon soy sauce
Salt
1 teaspoon sesame oil

A small piece of agar-agar
  (seaweed), or gelatine
2½ cups water or consommé
Cucumber
Tomato
Lettuce

Cook shrimps in boiling water with shredded ginger. Remove and season with soy sauce, salt, and sesame oil. Boil agar-agar with 2½ cups water until dissolved—about 15 minutes. Pour into a mould and add shrimps. Cool in the refrigerator for 1 to 1½ hours. When ready to serve turn out onto a plate and garnish with cucumber, sliced tomato, and lettuce.

FISH-STUFFED MUSHROOMS
YEUNG DOONG GWOO YEE

12 to 14 dried mushrooms
½ lb. fish fillets
Salt
A few ends of shallots, chopped

1 tablespoon soy sauce
1 egg white
Oil
1 tablespoon sugar
1 teaspoon sesame oil

Soak mushrooms in hot water for 20 minutes. Squeeze dry and remove stems. Mince fish fillets and combine with salt, soy sauce, and shallots. Bind with egg white. Heat pan, add oil, and sauté mushrooms for 2 minutes with sugar, sherry, and stock. Remove and cool. Pack fish filling on the underside of each mushroom and arrange in a shallow bowl with any liquor left over from mushrooms. Steam for 15 minutes. Before serving, sprinkle with sesame oil.
  Delicious when cold, too.

FISH ROE
YEE CHOON

½ lb. fish roes

1 egg

1 teaspoon soy sauce

Salt

Cornflour

Breadcrumbs

Oil for deep-frying

Lemon or lime slices

Beat egg lightly with soy sauce and salt. Cover fish roes with cornflour, dip in egg mixture, and then in breadcrumbs. Deep-fry in hot oil until golden brown. Drain on absorbent paper. Serve with wedges of lemon or lime.

SHRIMPS AND PINEAPPLE
BOR LOR HAR KOW

1 lb. raw whole shrimps

2 eggs

Salt

4 oz. plain flour

1 cup milk

Oil for deep-frying

1 inch green ginger

Pineapple pieces (canned)

Beat eggs together with a pinch of salt. Add sifted flour and enough of the milk to ensure a thin batter. Clean shrimps and remove head, tail, and shell. Slit back. Dip in batter. Heat pan, add oil and crushed ginger. Deep-fry shrimps. Remove, drain and arrange on a platter. Surround with pineapple pieces. Serve with Sweet-sour Sauce.

Sweet-sour sauce: Blend 2 teaspoons or more of arrowroot with a little water and add ¾ cup pineapple juice. Mix with 4 tablespoons sugar, 3 tablespoons vinegar, ½ teaspoon salt, and 1 teaspoon tomato sauce and bring to a boil. Simmer for one minute. Pour over fried shrimps and pineapple. Serve immediately.

SHRIMPS AND GREEN PEAS
CHING DOW HAR KOW

½ lb. shelled raw shrimps
1 cup green peas
4 tablespoons cornflour
8 teaspoons water
Oil for deep-frying

1 extra dessertspoon cornflour
2 tablespoons stock
2 tablespoons sherry
1 tablespoon soy sauce
Salt

Cook green peas in the usual way, saving the water to use as stock. Clean shrimps and split down the back. Mix cornflour with water to make a paste and cover shrimps with it. Deep-fry in oil. Drain. Remove most of the oil from the pan. Add cooked peas, return shrimps, and bind both with a sauce made with extra cornflour, stock from the peas, sherry, soy sauce, and salt to taste.

FISH ROLLS
YEE CHURN GURN

2 cups minced raw fish
4 dried mushrooms
1 onion
3 tablespoons minced cooked
  pork
A few green ends of shallots,
  chopped finely
1 tablespoon soy sauce

Salt
1 teaspoon sugar
Thin slices of ham or pork
  fat, as large as possible
2 eggs
Breadcrumbs
Oil for deep-frying

Prepare mushrooms by soaking in hot water for 20 minutes. Remove stems and chop finely. Peel onion and mince it, then mix together with fish, pork, and shallots. Season with soy sauce, salt, and sugar. Have pieces of ham or pork fat large enough to enclose filling, spread mixture on, and roll up as for spring rolls. Secure with a toothpick. Dip in beaten egg and then in breadcrumbs. Heat oil, then deep-fry rolls till brown. Drain on absorbent paper. Slice crosswise and serve hot.

STEAMED FISH
JING YEE

1 whole fish, about 2 lb.	1 inch green ginger, shredded
Salt and pepper	1 tablespoon crisp bacon
4 dried mushrooms	A few ends of shallots, chopped, or some Chinese parsley
1 teaspoon sugar	
1 tablespoon oil	
2 tablespoons soy sauce	

Prepare mushrooms by soaking for 20 minutes. Remove stems and shred. Clean fish, score with two incisions across fleshy part, and salt it inside and out. Sprinkle sugar on fish, pour on oil and soy sauce, and add ginger. Let stand for 10 minutes. Place mushrooms and bacon on top of fish and steam for 15 to 20 minutes. It can be baked in the oven protected by aluminium foil. Serve on a platter with a garnish of shallots or parsley.

SQUID WITH BEAN SPROUTS
NGAR CHOY CHOW YOW YEE

1 lb. fresh squid	1 tablespoon sherry
2 tablespoons oil	1 teaspoon sugar
1 clove garlic, crushed	Salt
1 inch green ginger, shredded	3 tablespoons stock
½ lb. bean sprouts	1 tablespoon thin oyster sauce
1 tablespoon cornflour	

Wash and clean squid thoroughly, removing the thin membrane. Slash inside crosswise and lengthwise, making a diamond pattern. Cut diagonally in pieces about 1½ inches long. Heat pan, add oil, garlic, and ginger, and sauté squid until it curls. Blanch bean sprouts and add to squid. Cook for a further minute. Bind with a sauce made from cornflour, sherry, sugar, salt, stock, and oyster sauce.

BRAISED SHARK'S FINS
CHIN PEI YEE CHEE

¼ lb. prepared shark's fins
½ cup cooked crabmeat
3 eggs
Salt
1 teaspoon monosodium glutamate

Oil
1 tablespoon lotus flour
1 tablespoon sherry
1 tablespoon soy sauce
1½ cups chicken stock
Extra crabmeat for a garnish

Soak the shark's fins in hot water for 30 minutes. Drain.
Shred crabmeat. Beat eggs lightly, add crabmeat, shark's
fins, salt, and monosodium glutamate. Put about 1 tablespoon of mixture on a porcelain spoon or egg cup and
steam for 30 minutes. Carefully turn out. Heat pan, add
oil, and gently fry the shark's fin. Make a sauce of lotus
flour, sherry, soy sauce, and chicken stock. Simmer for 5
minutes then add shark's fin, cooking for a further 5 minutes. Garnish with extra crabmeat and serve hot.

SHARK'S FIN SOUP
WART GAI YEE CHEE TONG

¼ lb. prepared shark's fin
1 breast of chicken
1 egg white
6 cups chicken stock
1 tablespoon soy sauce
1 tablespoon sherry

3 egg yolks
Salt
1 teaspoon monosodium glutamate
2 teaspoons lotus flour
Strips of cooked ham

Soak the shark's fins for 30 minutes in hot water. Drain.
Cut the breast of chicken in strips and mix with egg white.
Fry lightly. Bring chicken stock to a boil with shark's fins.
Simmer 10 minutes. Add chicken, soy sauce, sherry, egg
yolks, salt, and monosodium glutamate. Thicken with
blended lotus flour and simmer for a further 10 minutes.
Serve hot, with strips of ham on top.

KING PRAWN CUTLETS
JOW DAI HAR

12 raw king prawns	Breadcrumbs
2 eggs	Oil for deep-frying
1 teaspoon soy sauce	Lemon wedges
Salt	

Clean, peel, and shell prawns, leaving on tail-piece. With a sharp knife slit down the back of prawn, being careful not to cut right through. Remove any sand. Remove the vein. Beat eggs together with soy sauce and salt. Dip prawns in cornflour, egg mixture, and breadcrumbs. Press the cut side gently with the palm of the hand to flatten. Deep-fry in hot oil until golden brown. Drain on absorbent paper and serve with lemon wedges.

PRAWNS AND ASPARAGUS
LO SOON CHOW HAR KO

1½ lb. raw whole prawns	1 inch green ginger
1 bunch fresh asparagus	Salt
1 teaspoon sugar	1 teaspoon cornflour
2 tablespoons oil	2 tablespoons soy sauce

Wash and clean prawns, removing head, tail, and shell. Slice in half. Clean asparagus and cut into one-inch lengths (use tender stalks only). Cover with water, add sugar, and boil till tender. Remove, saving water for the sauce. Heat pan, add oil, salt, pepper, and crushed ginger. Sauté prawns until they turn pink. Add asparagus, mixing well together. Make a smooth paste with cornflour and 2 tablespoons asparagus water. Add soy sauce. Pour this sauce into the prawn mixture, then cook for a further 2 minutes with cover on.

*Sweet-sour Fish, a whole fish with crisp skin served with
sweet-sour sauce, mixed pickles added. Serve resting on a bed
of rice noodles, which represent seaweed.*

Stuffed Mushrooms (Yeung Doong Gwoo), a tasty morsel for cocktails; Spring Rolls (Chun Gurn), which can have various fillings; crisp Prawn Chips (Har Beang), ever popular, can be coloured for gala occasions; and Noodle Twists (Jow Wun Tun). A dish of Prawn Flowers would give an exotic touch to this hors-d'oeuvre selection.

STEAMED PRAWNS
JING HAR KO

1 lb. whole raw prawns	1 tablespoon oil
Salt	1 inch green ginger, shredded

Wash prawns and place them whole in a shallow bowl. Sprinkle with salt and oil. Place ginger on top of prawns. Steam for 15 minutes.

When cold these prawns may be peeled and served as a salad or an appetizer, or they may form the basis of many cooked dishes.

STEAMED WHOLE FISH WITH BLACK BEANS
DOW SEE JING YEE

1 whole fish, about 2 lb.	1 tablespoon preserved
Salt	Chinese black beans (dow
2 tablespoons soy sauce	see)
1 teaspoon sugar	1 tablespoon brandy
1 teaspoon sesame oil	1 inch green ginger, chopped
1 tablespoon vegetable oil	finely

Clean fish, leaving on head if desired for decorative purposes. Salt fish inside and out and score on fleshy part. Pour on soy sauce, sugar, and oils. Place on a deep plate. Mash beans with brandy and chopped ginger and spread this mixture over the fish. Steam for 15 minutes. Serve hot with plain rice.

STUFFED CRABS
YEUNG HAI HOCK

6 medium-sized uncooked crabs	6 water chestnuts
¼ lb. pork mince	1 egg
1 teaspoon soy sauce	Oil for deep-frying
Salt	1 inch green ginger, crushed
1 teaspoon sugar	Cucumbers
	Tomatoes

F

Stuffed Crabs—*Continued*.

Boil crabs and remove meat, leaving shells intact. Season pork mince with soy sauce, salt, and sugar. If chestnuts are fresh, peel skin, mince them and add to pork mince with the crabmeat. Mix in egg white. Pack this into well-cleaned crab-shells and brush over the top with beaten egg yolk. Steam for 10 minutes. Wipe the shells dry, heat oil and ginger, and deep-fry until top is brown. Drain. Serve with a garnish of cucumbers and tomatoes.

Instead of water chestnuts, try mincing a large onion and/or grating a large potato for a filling.

FISH CONGEE
YEE JOOK

1 lb. fish fillets	8 to 10 cups water
$\frac{3}{4}$ cup rice	A small quantity of cellophane noodles (jun see)
Salt	
2 inches green ginger	Oil for deep-frying
$\frac{1}{2}$ teaspoon monosodium glutamate	Sesame oil
	Shallots, chopped
A piece of preserved Chinese vegetable (choong choy)	Vegetable oil (hot)
	Soy sauce

Put rice, salt, and ginger into the water and bring to a boil. Add monosodium glutamate and simmer for about 2 hours. (Do not allow this congee to become too thick. If it does so, add more water.) Cut fish fillets into strips about 3 inches long. Wash choong choy and chop finely. Deep-fry cellophane noodles in hot oil and, when cool, crush gently. Into each soup bowl put 7 or 8 pieces of fish fillets and sprinkle with a little sesame oil; pour hot congee over fish; sprinkle on about $\frac{1}{4}$ teaspoon green onions, choong choy, vegetable oil, and soy sauce. Garnish with cellophane noodles. Serve with dip sauces—soy sauce, chilli sauce, or oyster sauce. A nice variation is to add toasted peanuts to the congee.

FISH SQUARES WITH
CRAB SAUCE
HAI JUP YEE

½ lb. fish fillets
Salt
1 teaspoon sesame oil
Cornflour
Oil for deep-frying

1 inch green ginger, crushed
1 extra tablespoon cornflour
½ cup fish stock
½ cup milk
Crabmeat

Cut fish into squares and sprinkle with salt. Add sesame oil and cover with cornflour on both sides. Deep-fry in hot oil seasoned with ginger. Drain and remove to a serving plate. For the sauce, blend 1 tablespoon cornflour and bring to a boil with stock and milk. Add crabmeat and stir well together. Pour over fish squares and serve hot. Garnish with Chinese parsley.

FRIED PRAWNS WITH
SWEET-SOUR SAUCE
SIN TIM HAR KO

1 lb. whole raw prawns
Oil or butter
Salt and pepper
1 clove garlic, crushed
1 inch green ginger, shredded
2 tablespoons arrowroot

2 teaspoons soy sauce
2 tablespoons vinegar
3 tablespoons sugar
2 teaspoons tomato sauce
2 cups pineapple juice

Remove head and tail of prawns, leaving the skin intact. Heat pan, add oil, salt, pepper, garlic, and ginger. Sauté prawns until they turn pink, then remove to a platter. For the sauce, mix arrowroot, soy sauce, vinegar, sugar, tomato sauce, juice, and ½ teaspoon salt together. Boil until it thickens. Return prawns to sauce and cook a further minute. Serve with a garnish of chillies or shallots.

SALT FISH
YIP HARM YEE

Have a whole fresh salmon, snapper, or carp about 2 lb.
Do not clean or remove inside fish. With a chopstick or
similar blunted stick push coarse salt through mouth.
Rub salt also on gills and around head. Stand fish upright
and pack with more salt until filled to capacity. Leave overnight lying in a flat position, holding down firmly with a
heavy stone. Next day, tie some string on the tail and cover
the fish in brown paper. Dry in the sun for 2 to 3 days. To
cook, cut fish in pieces, clean off fins, and remove the inside.
Place on a shallow dish, spread with shredded ginger, pour
over enough vegetable oil to moisten, and steam for 20 minutes.

This dish serves as an appetizer and is always accompanied by plain boiled rice—only very little of the fish is
eaten at one time.

SALT FISH
HARM YEE

A piece of salt fish (yip harm yee)	1 teaspoon sugar
Salt	A piece of green ginger, shredded
½ lb. pork mince	2 teaspoons vegetable oil

Season mince with salt and sugar. Form into a flat meat
cake. Place the salt fish and pork mince in a shallow bowl
and sprinkle shredded ginger on top. Pour vegetable oil
over top. Steam for 20 to 25 minutes. This is an appetizer
to be eaten with boiled rice.

WHOLE FISH
JUM TUE YEE

1 whole fish, very fresh, about 1 lb.	½ cup oil
Salt	2 inches green ginger, shredded
White ends of shallots	3 tablespoons soy sauce

Whole Fish—*Continued.*

Clean fish and salt it inside and out. Score with incisions through the fleshy part. Boil sufficient water to cover the fish, stand pan aside and immerse the fish in it for 10 to 15 minutes (depending on the thickness). Remove fish to a platter. Boil oil and ginger in another pan, then add soy sauce. Surround fish with shallot flowers (the ends are stripped with a sharp knife and covered with cold water for 10 minutes, when they will curl backwards). Pour the boiling oil over the fish so that it will sizzle and crisp the skin.

FISH CHOP SUEY
YEE JUP SUI

1 lb. fish fillets	1 teaspoon sugar
Salt	½ cup water
Cornflour	1 capsicum
Oil for deep-frying	2 teaspoons cornflour
1 onion	½ cup fish stock
1 clove garlic	1 teaspoon oyster sauce
1 cup green beans	(optional)

Cut fish fillets into squares about an inch in size. Salt and sprinkle with cornflour. Deep-fry in hot oil. Drain. Heat pan, add a little oil, and sauté cut-up onion. Remove. Add more oil, then garlic, and when it is brown put beans in (cut into pieces). Season with salt and sugar and sauté for one minute. Pour in water and simmer with lid on for a further 2 minutes. Remove and save liquor. Put fish, onion, beans, and cut-up capsicum in the pan and mix till heated. Blend cornflour with liquor from beans, mix in stock and oyster sauce, and cook together with mixture for 1½ minutes.

GOLDEN FISH WITH SWEET-SOUR SAUCE
TIM SIN GUM YUE

1 whole fish, about 2 lb.
Salt
4 egg yolks
Cornflour
Oil for deep-frying
½ cup sugar

½ cup vinegar
1 cup melon liquor or pine-apple juice
1 cup melon shred (gwah ying)
Rice noodles (mei fun)

Clean and wash fish, dry thoroughly, and salt it all over. Score fish on each side. Brush on beaten egg yolks, then dip into cornflour. Shake off excess. Heat oil in a deep pan and baste gashes with oil by holding head or tail end on side of pan, then deep-fry until golden brown and cooked through thickest part of fish. Remove, drain, and lift onto a platter. For the sauce, boil together the sugar, vinegar, and melon liquor and thicken with blended cornflour. Add melon shred and heat through. Pour this sauce over the fish, and surround with fried noodles.

CURRIED PRAWNS
GAR LEE HAR

1½ to 2 lb. raw prawns
3 tablespoons oil
1 clove garlic, crushed
Salt and pepper
1 inch green ginger, shredded
1 tablespoon curry powder or
   1 teaspoon curry paste
   (according to taste)

2 onions
1 potato
1 cup water
1 cup coconut milk
1 tablespoon butter or mar-garine
1 tablespoon flour

Wash, peel, and shell prawns. Split down the back, removing any sand and the black vein. Heat the pan, add oil, garlic, salt, pepper, and ginger. Sauté prawns until they turn pink. Remove. Add a little more oil if necessary and sauté sliced onions until soft. Add curry powder and/or

Curried Prawns—*Continued.*

curry paste, cut-up potato, and water. Cover with lid and simmer until potato is cooked. Blend butter with flour and pour in gradually the coconut milk, which has been boiled. (To make coconut milk pour boiling water over desiccated coconut strained through a muslin cloth; or use fresh coconut, in which case mince the coconut meat first.) Pour this into curry mixture, together with prawns, and cook a further 3 minutes. Serve hot with fluffy white rice.

Cooked prawns may be used, and introduced after the potatoes are cooked. Remember that when the shells, tail, and head are removed from 1 lb. of cooked prawns, only about 6 oz. of food remain.

CRISP SKIN FISH WITH PINEAPPLE SAUCE
CHOI PEE YEE

1 whole fish, about 2 lb.	1 egg
Salt	Breadcrumbs
Soy sauce	Oil for deep-frying
Cornflour	

Split fish in half lengthwise from top edge, removing backbone. Season with salt and soy sauce and sprinkle with cornflour. Brush on beaten egg, cover with breadcrumbs, and deep-fry in hot oil, keeping the whole fish flat to prevent the edges curling up. Drain and remove to a platter.

Fresh pineapple sauce: Cut pineapple into triangular pieces and cover with water. When boiling, add sugar to taste, then simmer until pineapple softens. Add 1 teaspoon sweet vinegar and $\frac{1}{2}$ teaspoon salt. Thicken with 1 teaspoon cornflour and cook for a further 2 minutes. Pour this over the whole fish. Garnish with fried pineapple (the pieces are dipped in beaten egg, then in breadcrumbs, and deep-fried).

8

Noodles

NOODLE DISHES are so popular in Far Eastern countries that they are eaten at any hour of the day or night, and vendors selling noodles in the street are as common a sight as the ice-cream man. Noodles are made with the flour of wheat, rice, or bean, mixed with eggs and other ingredients, and coloured for special occasions. They are obtainable both fresh and dehydrated. Every shape and size of noodles imaginable is made, and they are a versatile food, combining with any ingredient so successfully that they are found in an amazing variety of dishes—fried, boiled, sautéd, braised, used in soups and also as a garnish. The ones made with bean flour are of fine texture, crisp—some are even transparent, being known as cellophane noodles. Noodles are a symbol of Long Life and are always served on the celebration of a birthday. A Noodle Party given by a westernized hostess may impart that exotic touch to her next birthday celebration.

When eating noodles, chopsticks and a spoon are used. The noodles should be cooked correctly—they must be soft in the centre and yet be firm enough to snap at a manageable length for gracious eating.

It is known that Marco Polo discovered noodles in the thirteenth century whilst on an exploring expedition to China, and he was so impressed with this basic food that he introduced it to European countries, where the product became known as spaghetti and macaroni. The difference with Chinese noodles is that when cooked they increase a half their original bulk, whereas spaghetti and similar products become doubled in quantity when cooked—a point to keep in mind when calculating the amount for each serving.

NOODLE PASTE
GAI DARN MEIN

1 lb. strong flour	3 or 4 eggs
½ teaspoon salt	Cornflour

Sift flour and salt together onto a pastry board (strong flour has a high gluten content). Make a well and break in the unbeaten eggs. Make into a dough. Sprinkle the board with cornflour and knead the paste, brushing off excess cornflour. Roll out until transparent, and cut into desired lengths.

This recipe is also suitable for making the skins for wun tuns.

SHORT SOUP
WUN TUN

Noodle paste, cut into 2½-inch squares	6 dried mushrooms
½ lb. pork mince (not too lean)	Salt
	2 teaspoons soy sauce
	1 egg white
½ lb. raw shelled prawns	

Prepare mushrooms by soaking in hot water for 20 minutes. Mince together with pork and prawns. Season with salt and soy sauce, binding together with egg white. Place about one teaspoon of the mixture on each square and wrap in tightly, if necessary sealing the edges with beaten egg.

These can be added to hot soup and served alone, or with plain egg noodles, when the dish is known as Long and Short Soup.

DIM SIMS

¼ lb. pork mince (not too lean)
2 oz. lard
¼ lb. raw shelled prawns
4 prepared dried mushrooms
Salt and pepper

1 teaspoon sugar
2 teaspoons soy sauce
2 tablespoons minced water chestnuts
Noodle paste, made into thin 3-inch squares

Mince all the ingredients together and season. Put a teaspoon of filling in the centre of each noodle square and roughly wrap around. Fill in the top with a small shrimp, and steam for 30 minutes.

STEAMED PATTY
FUN GOR

½ lb. Chinese flour (deng min fun)

A pinch of salt
Hot water, ½ to 2 cups

Place flour and salt in a bowl. Using a wooden spoon gradually mix in hot water sufficient to make into a firm dough. Knead lightly when warm, and keep covered with a clean cloth. Take out half the quantity and form it into a long roll about one inch in diameter, cut it about half an inch thick and roll into a small ball. With a greased cleaver, press the ball of dough to form a circle. This is the skin or patty, ready to take the filling.

Filling

½ lb. cooked prawns
¾ cup diced bamboo shoots
3 tablespoons diced ham or pork fat

1 tablespoon soy sauce
Salt and pepper
½ teaspoon monosodium glutamate

Mix chopped up prawns, bamboo shoots, and ham fat in a bowl, and season with soy sauce, salt, and pepper, and monosodium glutamate. Knead together lightly. Place about 2 teaspoons of this filling on each patty, and make

Steamed Patty—*Continued.*

six or seven pleats on top to enclose the filling. Steam by the indirect steaming method for approximately 15 minutes.

PLAIN FRIED NOODLES
JOW MEIN

Have 1 lb. fresh egg noodles and enough oil for deep-frying. Heat oil at a moderate temperature, and place noodles in a little at a time, separating them so that they will colour evenly and be quite crisp. Drain. (When a piece of noodle is dropped into the oil and immediately rises to the top, then the oil is the correct temperature for deep-frying— about 370 degrees F.)

PRAWN CHOW MEIN
HAR CHOW MEIN

½ lb. fresh egg noodles	1 lb. raw shelled prawns
Oil for deep-frying	1 large onion
2 eggs	8 mushrooms, cooked
Salt	10 water chestnuts
1 cup green beans, or a small bunch of Chinese cabbage	¾ cup stock
	1 tablespoon soy sauce
1 inch green ginger, shredded	1 tablespoon cornflour

Deep-fry noodles in hot oil until crisp. Drain, and remove to a platter. Beat seasoned eggs lightly and make into a thin omelette. When cold, cut into 2-inch strips. Parboil semi-hard vegetables (beans or cabbage). Heat pan, add oil and ginger, and sauté prawns until they turn pink. Remove. Add a little more oil, then sauté sliced onion, mushrooms, beans and chestnuts. Return prawns and mix in with the vegetables, cooking for another minute. Pour in stock and soy sauce and thicken with blended cornflour cooking for a further 2 minutes. Pour mixture over fried noodles, and sprinkle with shredded egg.

BRAISED NOODLES
WOR MEIN

½ lb. lean pork
8 mushrooms
1 tablespoon fungi (chee yee)
1 large onion
A piece of bamboo shoot
1 tablespoon cornflour

3 tablespoons soy sauce
Oil or lard
3 stalks blanched Chinese
vegetable (gai larn)
½ cup stock
½ lb. rice noodles (sar ho fun)

Soak mushrooms (if dried) and fungi in hot water for 20 minutes. Slice onion, bamboo shoot, mushrooms, and pork thinly. Blend cornflour and add soy sauce (to be used for thickening). Heat pan, add oil, and sauté the pork. Add more oil if necessary, then fry onion, fungi, mushrooms, Chinese vegetable, and bamboo shoot, mixing thoroughly. Make a well in the centre of the mixture and pour in stock. Cover with a lid and simmer for 2 minutes. Add blended cornflour, cook a further minute, and serve over cooked rice noodles. To cook them, soak the dried noodles in cold water for 10 minutes, then cook in salted boiling water for 20 minutes. Drain and run cold water through immediately.

SHORT SOUP WITH SWEET-SOUR SAUCE
GOO LOO WUN TUN

20 wun tuns
Oil for deep-frying
½ lb. shelled raw prawns

½ lb. roast pork (char sui)
1 cup mixed pickled vegetables

Deep-fry wun tuns and set aside. Heat pan and cook prawns, mix in sliced pork and vegetables. Add to wun tuns, arrange on a platter, and pour over the following sauce: combine ½ cup sugar, ½ cup vinegar, 1 cup pineapple juice or pickle juice, 1 inch green ginger, 1 teaspoon sherry, a pinch of salt, and 1 tablespoon blended cornflour and stir over heat until boiling.

FRIED NOODLE MIXTURE
SUB GUM CHOW MEIN

½ lb. fresh egg noodles
½ lb. pork
2 tablespoons soy sauce
1 tablespoon sugar
Salt
½ teaspoon monosodium glutamate
5 dried mushrooms
2 stalks celery
1 medium-size onion

A piece of bamboo shoot
2 stalks Chinese cabbage, or
1 cup Chinese peas in the pod
1 carrot
Oil for deep-frying
¾ cup stock
1 tablespoon cornflour
1 tablespoon oyster sauce
2 tablespoons sesame seeds

Cut pork into thin slices. Season with soy sauce, sugar, salt, and monosodium glutamate. Let stand for 15 minutes. Prepare mushrooms and slice together with celery, onion, bamboo shoot, Chinese cabbage, and carrot. Heat pan, add oil, and sauté pork until it turns colour, then add vegetables moistened with stock. Cook 3 minutes, mixing well together. Add stock and cook a further minute. Thicken with blended cornflour and oyster sauce, cooking for another minute. Deep-fry noodles, drain, and arrange on a platter. Pour mixture over fried noodles and sprinkle with toasted sesame seeds.

VELVET NOODLES WITH BEEF
KNO YUK EE MEIN

½ lb. fine fresh egg noodles
½ lb. beef
2 tablespoons soy sauce
Salt and pepper
Oil
1 clove garlic

1 inch green ginger
1 small bunch Chinese cabbage (gai larn)
¾ cup stock
Shallots
1 tablespoon chestnut flour

Put noodles into boiling water, loosen, and cook for 3 minutes. Drain. Slice beef and season with soy sauce, salt, and pepper. Heat pan, add a little oil, then the garlic and green ginger, crushed. Sauté beef until brown. Parboil sliced

Velvet Noodles with Beef—*Continued.*

Chinese cabbage, add to beef. Pour in stock and simmer for 2 minutes. Add shallots, which have been cut into strips. Mix chestnut flour with water, add to mixture, and stir until thickened. Stir this mixture into the cooked noodles and serve immediately.

SPRING ROLLS
CHUN GURN

2 cups plain flour
1 cup cornflour
$\frac{1}{4}$ teaspoon salt
1 egg (optional)
2 cups water (approx.)
$\frac{1}{2}$ lb. pork mince
2 teaspoons soy sauce
1 teaspoon sugar

$\frac{1}{2}$ teaspoon monosodium glutamate
8 dried mushrooms
12 water chestnuts
1 cup shredded Chinese soft vegetable (wong ah bark)
1 cup sliced cooked chicken
1 egg white
Oil for deep-frying

For the skins, sift together flour, cornflour, and $\frac{1}{4}$ teaspoon salt. Mix in beaten egg and add water slowly to make a light thin batter. Strain. Let stand for one hour. Grease pan lightly and pour in a thin layer of batter, to make pancake about 6 to 7 inches in diameter. Cook until lightly browned on one side only. Cool.

To make the filling, season pork mince with soy sauce, sugar, salt, and monosodium glutamate. Prepare mushrooms by soaking in hot water for 20 minutes, and, when ready, chop finely together with water chestnuts. Add to seasoned pork and mix well together. Cook lightly in a little oil and mix in shredded vegetable. Cool and drain off any liquid. Place pork mixture on cooked side of skin, and top with a slice of chicken. Brush edges with beaten egg white, and wrap into a neat parcel, tucking in the ends securely. Deep-fry in hot oil until golden brown all over. Drain on absorbent paper.

The filling can be varied by using mincemeat, bean sprouts, shredded cabbage, seafoods, etc.

9

 Rice

AN ANCIENT CHINESE SCRIPT records the sowing of rice as an annual religious ceremonial of five thousand years ago, and Chinese classics describe a system of rice irrigation constructed by Emperor Yu about 2356 B.C.

A bowl of rice means Life itself, and is looked upon with reverence by the Chinese. It is used when hot as an accompaniment to a meal, and no Chinese meal is ever served without it. Left to cool completely, or till the next day, it can be made up into a dish of fried rice, which successfully combines with left-over titbits and is very suitable as a breakfast treat. Plain cold rice can be reheated by placing it in a deep bowl and steaming it, or adding a little water to the rice in a pot and heating over a slow fire until warm.

At a meal, the rice bowl is held in the left hand with the thumb resting on the rim, while the base is held firmly with the other fingers; using chopsticks, it is easy to convey the rice to the mouth. All the grains in the bowl must be eaten, for it is unforgivable in Chinese eyes to leave any rice at the bottom of the rice bowl—it is, in fact, regarded as an insult to your host to do so. If the initial bowl contains too much, then it is permissible to request a smaller serve.

If you mix a little butter and soy sauce into a bowl of hot steamed rice, it becomes the Chinese equivalent of mashed potatoes and gravy. Rice should always be washed three or four times in cold water before it is cooked or until the last lot of water remains clear. Depending on the quality of the rice and on personal preference, it is usual to have equivalent parts of water and rice; or cover the rice with cold water to come three-quarters of an inch over the rice level in the saucepan. This is brought to a boil, then the heat is reduced, and when all the water has evaporated and air bubbles show, immediately reduce the heat to the lowest degree, cover with a tight-fitting lid, and allow to steam. There is another type of rice, nor mei; which is glutinous and used for making different varieties of sweet and salty cakes and puddings.

Either of the following methods is suitable for boiling rice that is then to be fried, or is to be stored in a refrigerator. Instead of water, cook rice in chicken stock, meat stock, or coconut milk for added flavour.

PLAIN BOILED RICE 1

Wash 1 lb. rice in cold water three or four times, or until water is clear. Add cold water to come approximately three-quarters of an inch above rice level. Bring to a boil, then reduce the heat to medium and continue cooking until all the water has evaporated and air bubbles show. Immediately reduce the heat to the lowest, cover with a tight-fitting lid, and simmer for 15 to 20 minutes. It is not necessary to stir the rice at all during this process.

PLAIN BOILED RICE 2

Wash 3 cups rice in cold water three or four times or until water is clear. Add 3 cups cold water and bring to a boil quickly. When the water has evaporated, immediately reduce the heat to the lowest, cover with a tight-fitting lid, and simmer for 20 minutes. (It may be necessary to use a little more water for thin-grained rice.)

Special Fried Rice, a meal by itself. It is shown here with a garnish of Chinese parsley and cooked whole prawns.

Cucumber Soup (Gwah Tong), page 38, makes a well-balanced meal in itself.

BASIC FRIED RICE
CHOW FARN

3 cups cooked rice, cold
2 slices bacon
1½ tablespoons oil
2 or 3 eggs
Salt to taste

Shallots or chives
½ teaspoon monosodium
glutamate
1 tablespoon soy sauce

This recipe is used as an accompaniment to another dish. Shred bacon and cook until crisp. Discard drippings. Heat pan, add oil and pour in beaten eggs. Before the eggs set, add rice quickly, salt to taste, and work the rice into the egg mixture. Add bacon, chopped shallots, monosodium glutamate, and sprinkle on the soy sauce, turning frequently.

BOILED RICE AND CHINESE SALAMI
LARP CHOONG FARN

1 lb. rice
2½ cups water

2 small pairs Chinese salami

Wash rice in cold water three or four times or until water is clear. Cover with the cold water and bring to a boil until the water has evaporated. Reduce heat immediately to the lowest, and place Chinese salami (which has been wiped with a warm damp cloth) on top of the rice; cover with a tight-fitting lid and steam for approximately 20 minutes. Garnish with Chinese parsley.

FRIED RICE WITH HAM
FOR TOI CHOW FARN

3 cups cold cooked rice
2 tablespoons oil
1 large onion
Salt

2 eggs
2 slices cooked ham
Shallots, chopped
1 tablespoon soy sauce

G

Fried Rice with Ham—*Continued.*

Heat pan, add oil, and fry sliced onion until slightly brown. Add rice and salt. Make a well in centre, pour in beaten eggs and fold in rice. Fry, stirring constantly for a few minutes, then add sliced ham and the shallots. Sprinkle on the soy sauce, mix in well, and serve hot. Spoon hot rice into a fluted mould, turn out on a platter, and surround with extra pieces of ham or pieces of sweet pineapple.

FRIED RICE WITH CRAB
HAI CHOW FARN

3 cups cold cooked rice	Salt
2 tablespoons oil	$\frac{1}{4}$ lb. cooked crabmeat
1 medium-sized onion	Shallots, chopped
3 eggs	1 tablespoon soy sauce

Heat pan, add oil, and fry shredded onion. Beat eggs together and pour into pan, adding a little extra oil. When almost set, pour in rice and salt, mixing so that the egg coats the rice. Add flaked crabmeat and shallots and sprinkle with soy sauce. Cook through until heated, stirring constantly.

STEAMED RICE WITH CHICKEN
GAI KO FARN

1 small chicken, about 2 lb.	1 inch green ginger, crushed
1 tablespoon soy sauce	2 cups rice
Salt	3 cups water
1 tablespoon sherry	

Clean and wash chicken. Cut into large pieces about 2 inches through the bone and season with soy sauce, salt, sherry, and ginger. Let stand for 15 minutes. Wash rice and put it into a saucepan with the water. Bring to a boil, then add pieces of chicken and simmer until the water has evaporated. Steam over low heat for 30 minutes. Serve hot with oyster dip sauce.

RICE WITH BEEF SLICES
KNO YUK FARN

½ lb. lean beef	2 teaspoons cornflour
1½ tablespoons soy sauce	2 tablespoons oil
1 clove garlic	3 cups cooked rice
1 inch green ginger	2 eggs
Salt	1 cup chicken stock

Slice beef in thin strips and season with soy sauce, chopped garlic, sliced ginger, salt, and cornflour. Heat pan, add oil, and fry until brown. Add rice, mixing in thoroughly. Make a well in the centre, adding more oil if required, and pour in beaten eggs. Mix rice in, stirring frequently. Pour in chicken stock and simmer for 5 minutes. Serve hot with a garnish of Chinese parsley.

RICE WITH RED BEANS
HOONG DOW FARN

4 tablespoons red beans (hoong dow)	5 cups water
¼ lb. rice	5 tablespoons sugar

Soak beans overnight in warm water. Wash and rinse in a few changes of water. Put beans and rice in a large saucepan with water, bring to a boil, and simmer for 1 to 1½ hours. Add sugar before serving.

This is served as a snack for convalescents or invalids.

RICE BUTTER AND SOY SAUCE
BUTTA SEE YO FARN

1 cup hot steamed rice	1 teaspoon soy sauce
2 teaspoons butter	

Melt butter into hot rice and then mix in soy sauce.

FRIED RICE WITH
SHRIMP PASTE
HARM HAR FARN

4 cups cooked rice   Salt
1 fillet cooked pork (char sui)   1 teaspoon shrimp paste
3 eggs   (harm har)
Oil   Shallots, chopped

Cut pork into small dice size and add to beaten eggs. Heat
pan, add oil and pour in egg-pork mixture. Stir well so that
the mixture is in individual pieces, and as the egg sets on
the diced pork, add rice, salt, shrimp paste, and shallots.
Shrimp paste is very salty, so be careful with the salt. Keep
turning mixture over rapidly to fry to brownness desired.

LOBSTER FRIED RICE
DAI HAR CHOW FARN

4 cups cold cooked rice   3 eggs
1 cup bean sprouts   Salt
Oil   1 cup cooked lobster meat
1 inch green ginger, shredded   Chopped shallots
1 teaspoon sugar   1 tablespoon soy sauce

Clean and wash bean sprouts. Heat pan, add oil and ginger,
and sauté bean sprouts for one minute, with sugar added.
Remove and drain off liquor. Make a thin omelette with
beaten eggs. When cool, cut into shreds. Clean and reheat
pan, add oil, then fry rice with salt to taste until heated
through. Add cut-up lobster, bean sprouts, and shallots,
mixing well together and turning all the time. Sprinkle
with soy sauce and continue frying until it is the desired
brownness. Serve very hot with the shredded egg placed on
top of the fried rice. Garnish with lettuce.

MUSHROOM FRIED RICE
DOONG GWOO CHOW FARN

3 cups cold cooked rice   Salt
8 dried mushrooms   3 slices cooked ham
1 medium-sized onion   Chopped shallots
3 eggs   1 tablespoon soy sauce
2 tablespoons oil

Prepare mushrooms by soaking in hot water for 20 minutes. Shred finely. Slice onion, and sauté until soft. Make a thin omelette with beaten eggs, and when cool cut into shreds. Clean pan, reheat, add oil, and sauté mushrooms for 2 minutes. Add rice, salt to taste, and continue to fry briskly, mixing in shredded ham, onions, shallots, and soy sauce when well heated through. Garnish with shredded egg and serve at once.

PEKING-STYLE FRIED RICE
BUKIN CHOW FARN

4 cups cold cooked rice   Salt
½ cup olive nuts (larm yin)   3 slices cooked ham
   or almonds   Shallots, chopped
Oil   1 tablespoon soy sauce
4 eggs

Toast nuts in hot oil. Beat eggs together with salt to taste. Shred ham. Heat pan, add oil and pour in eggs. When half set, add rice and salt, stirring rapidly so that the egg starts to coat the grains of rice. Add ham and shallots and sprinkle with soy sauce, mixing all well together. Keep frying the rice until the required brownness is reached. Serve sprinkled with the olive nuts or slivered almonds.

GINGER RICE
GEUNG FARN

2 cups rice
2½ cups water
½ teaspoon salt

A pinch of saffron
½ cup ginger in syrup
A knob of butter

Wash rice and bring to a boil with water, salt, and saffron. Drain ginger and add to rice when water has evaporated. Turn heat to lowest and simmer for 15 minutes. Put a knob of butter on top and with a fork mix it into the rice. Spoon hot rice into a fluted mould. Unmould on a platter. Serve hot.

 **Dessert**

IT IS NOT because the Chinese palate does not appreciate desserts and sweets that they do not appear in such great profusion as on the westernized menu, but because of the lack of ovens in the average Chinese home. In olden times most Chinese people relied on the special cake shops to provide the sweet course, but today, with the progress made in developing cooking appliances for the home, and the return to their homeland of overseas Chinese, desserts are fast becoming popular on the Chinese menu. However, the Chinese have always had their special-occasion cakes, which vary in shape and size, containing sweet, salty, and nutty fillings. Round cakes, usually 4 inches in diameter and one inch high, containing an astonishing combination of flavours, decorated with red characters on top, are the special feature of the Moon Festival, which is celebrated on the fifteenth day of the Eighth Moon (some time in September). It is reported that the moon shines brightest on this date, and so the cakes are baked in a round shape, this symbolizing completeness and fulfilment and are readily consumed by all with these thoughts in mind.

In the event of a wedding taking place, both families exchange gifts of small round glutinous rice-flour cakes with sweet bean paste fillings, and these are also distributed to those who send wedding presents.

At the end of a banquet menu, dessert could consist of fresh fruit only, but there is a selection ranging from glutinous rice puddings to steamed cakes and egg custards to choose from, if desired. In a family affair, there would probably be only fresh fruits, iced desserts, or candied sweetmeats.

ALMOND COOKIES
HUNG YUN BEANG

3 cups plain flour	1 egg
1 teaspoon baking powder	1 teaspoon almond essence
½ teaspoon salt	1 teaspoon almond powder
½ lb. shortening	Blanched almonds
1 cup sugar	Red colouring

Sift flour, baking powder, and salt together. Cream shortening with sugar until fluffy, add beaten egg and almond essence gradually. Add almond powder to sifted flour, and mix into beaten egg mixture to form a firm dough. With floured hands roll small pieces into balls and place them apart on a greased tray. Place an almond on top of each cookie and glaze with slightly beaten egg. Instead of using an almond, an indent could be made on top with a chopstick dipped in red colouring. Bake in a moderate oven for 20 minutes.

MOONSTONES
DAI CHOY GO

2 oz. agar-agar	½ cup sugar
4 cups cool water, or fruit syrup (preferably)	1 teaspoon lemon essence
	Red colouring

Rinse the agar-agar in water first if necessary. Soak in cool water or fruit syrup for 10 minutes. Add sugar and bring to a boil. Continue to boil until the agar-agar is completely dissolved. Remove, add lemon essence. Pour half into a mould and let it cool. Use a few drops of red colouring in

Moonstones—*Continued.*

the remainder, pour into another mould, and let it cool. When set, cut into small squares or scoop out into round ball shapes. Serve in tall glasses with a mixture of both.

PEANUT BRITTLE
FARR SHUNG TONG

2 cups brown sugar   1 tablespoon water
3 tablespoons vinegar   ½ lb. shelled peanuts

Bring sugar, vinegar, and water to a boil. Simmer until the syrup is thick and becomes brittle (approximately 240 degrees) when a little is dropped into cold water. Oil a cake tin with peanut oil and sprinkle with cooked peanuts. Pour the syrup over the peanuts, spreading evenly and smoothing with a flat utensil. Before the sweet is cold, cut into desired lengths. Store in an air-tight container.

NEW YEAR DUMPLINGS
JIN DOIH

½ cup brown sugar   1 cup white sugar
1 cup water   Sesame seeds
1 lb. rice flour (nor mai fun)   Oil for deep-frying
1 lb. red beans (hoong dow)

Dissolve brown sugar in water by stirring slowly over low heat. Allow to cool. Put rice flour into a bowl, make a well in the centre, and add brown sugar syrup slowly. Mix and then knead until stiff. To make the filling, cook beans and white sugar in water, simmering for 2 hours or until beans are soft, adding extra water if necessary. Mash the beans through a strainer or through muslin cloth. Take about 2 tablespoons of dough and flatten gently on the palm of the hand, put in one teaspoon of filling, cover over and form into a round ball. Dip into sesame seeds. Deep-fry in hot oil until brown. Drain on absorbent paper.

NEW YEAR PUDDING
YEAH JEE GOH

3 cups water
1½ lb. brown sugar
1 lb. rice flour (nor mai fun)
1½ tablespoons vegetable oil

½ cup finely shredded fresh
  coconut
3 or 4 red dates
2 teaspoons toasted sesame
  seeds

Boil water and sugar together until sugar has dissolved.
Cool. Put rice flour into a deep bowl and gradually pour in
syrup and oil, mixing well. Stir in coconut. Line a round
tin (about 8 inches in diameter) with greased bamboo
or banana leaves, pour in mixture, top with sliced red dates,
and sprinkle with sesame seeds. Steam for 4 to 5 hours. This
dessert is eaten cold and may be sliced and then fried in a
little oil, or dipped into beaten egg and fried.
  Variations: Use fresh chestnut pulp, grated white turnips, or a few slices of salted pork pieces as fillings.

MEDICINAL HERBS
TIM CHUN POR LOONG

½ lb. medicinal herbs (chun
  por loong)
2 pints water (approx.)

1 cup Chinese rock sugar
  (beng tong)
1 egg

Boil herbs and water together, add sugar, and simmer for
1¼ hours. Break in an egg and mix thoroughly. Serve in
separate bowls with extra sugar to sweeten, if desired.

SOY SAUCE COCONUT
SEE YO YEAH JEE

Break open a fresh coconut and take out the flesh with a
sharp knife. Scrap off the dark hard skin and slice the white
flesh in strips. Cover with plenty of water and soy sauce
(half and half). Bring to a boil, then simmer for one hour
or until the flavour of the sauce penetrates the flesh. Drain
and serve as a sweet candy.

SWEET RICE
CHAR MEI

½ lb. Chinese brown slab sugar

4 cups rice breakfast cereal, or glutinous rice (nor mei)

1 tablespoon water (approx.)

A 2-inch piece of green ginger

1 teaspoon vinegar

Melt sugar very slowly in a saucepan with enough water to moisten. When it becomes liquid and has reached toffee-setting stage when tested in cold water (approximately 280 degrees), pour in rice cereal, mix vigorously, then add ginger (cut into fine strips) and vinegar. Pour onto a greased tin, and mark out into desired lengths before the mixture hardens.

STEAMED BUNS
CHAR SUI BOW

1½ cups warm water

2 tablespoons sugar

1½ tablespoons oil

Salt

1 oz. yeast

1¼ lb. plain flour

Place water, sugar and oil in a mixing bowl. Dissolve yeast in ½ cup warm water and add to mixture. (Temperature between 78°F. and 82°F. is the most suitable for fermentation.) Stir in sifted flour. Knead well to a dough that will not stick to the hands. Remove to a floured board and knead again. Place the dough in a bowl and allow to rise until double in bulk (about 1½ to 2 hours). Knead down, and take off enough dough to form into a small bun. Fill with barbecued pork mixture, close over, and make a slightly pointed top. With a blunt pointed instrument or chopstick, dip into red colouring and dot the point. Cut a small piece of greaseproof paper for the base of the bun, let it stand for another hour, and then steam for 30 minutes.

Steamed Buns—*Continued.*

Filling

2 tablespoons brown bean   1 teaspoon vegetable oil
  paste (min see jeung)   ½ lb. red roast pork (char sui)

Mash brown beans in a bowl, and fry gently with oil until smooth and flowing. Dice cooked pork and mix into sauce. Allow to cool, and spoon into dough.

ALMOND TEA
HUNG YUN CHAR

½ cup ground almond powder   ¾ cup unsweetened evapor-
1 tablespoon lotus flour   ated milk
½ cup sugar   4 cups water
                             Slivers of toasted almonds

Combine ground almond powder, lotus flour, and sugar in a saucepan. Add milk and water very gradually. Bring to a boil, stirring constantly, and let simmer for 10 minutes. Serve hot in a small basin sprinkled with toasted slivers of almonds.

INDEX